BOOK PUBLISHING
INSTRUCTIONS

A Step-by-Step Guide to Publishing Your Book
as a Paperback and eBook

Book Publishing Instructions

*A Step-by-Step Guide to Publishing Your Book
as a Paperback and eBook*

Jeremy Myers

BOOK PUBLISHING INSTRUCTIONS:
A Step-by-Step Guide to Publishing Your Book as a Paperback and eBook
© 2013 by Jeremy Myers

Published by Redeeming Press
Dallas, OR 97338
RedeemingPress.com

Discover other titles by Jeremy Myers at TillHeComes.org

Get future eBooks from Jeremy Myers for free by signing up to receive his email newsletter at www.tillhecomes.org/subscribe/

ISBN: 978-1-939992-16-1 (Paperback)
ISBN: 978-1-939992-17-8 (Mobi)
ISBN: 978-1-939992-18-5 (ePub)

For my wife, Wendy.

Thanks for reading everything I write
and remaining my number one fan.

TABLE OF CONTENTS

INTRODUCTION

Never before in the history of the world has it been so easy for new and undiscovered authors to break into print. This means that you can get your book published. Yes, you can get your book into print *this year!* Whether you have a novel or a non-fiction book on history, theology, poetry, or even favorite family recipes, it is now easier than ever before to get your book into the hands of readers around the world.

This book is going to show you how.

But before I do that, I have a warning about this book and how it differs from other books like it on the market. There are thousands of other books just like this one. I have read dozens of them. Most of those books try to pad their page-count and keep readers interested with things like anecdotes, inspiring quotes, success stories of self-published authors, and high-flying promises that if you just follow the steps in their book (and buy into their publishing program for only $599), then you too can be a best-selling author.

I am not going to do any of that in this book. None of it.

This book is so straight-forward, I am not even going to waste space telling you who I am, what I do for a living, or how I am qualified to write this book. For those of you who want this information, I will include a brief page at the end of this book which provides some of those details.

In other words, this book is going to be a dull, drab, boring, just-the-facts, down-and-dirty "how to" book. It is simply going to provide step-by-step instructions for preparing your manuscript for publication in the expanding eBook market worldwide. I will even throw in a few tips and suggestions on how to prepare your manuscript for printing as a paperback book, and how to get people to read and buy your book.

This book is not intended to encourage you to write a book. I assume that you already have written one or that you want to write one. This book is not designed to set up false expectations for how many books you might be able to sell. You will probably sell less than 100. But if you are an author, you don't care. True authors write for the joy of writing and to get their ideas out on paper. So if that describes you, then this book might be for you as well. You don't want the fluff. You just want a simple, step-by-step guide to getting your book published. Each chapter begins with a few introductory paragraphs about the content of the chapter, with the remainder of the chapter being written in a checklist format so that as you prepare your book for publication, you can literally follow the steps one-by-one and check them off as you go. To get a free quick-start publishing guide based on the content of this book, I will send one when you sign up for the free Redeeming Press newsletter.

One final note: I use the following software programs to prepare my books for publication. Other similar tools and programs are available, but those may not have the same functionality as represented in this guide.

- Typing, Editing, and Typesetting the Manuscript: Microsoft Word
- Blogging and Websites: Wordpress.org and the Genesis Framework
- Book Cover Design: Adobe Photoshop
- HTML and ePub editor: Notepad++
- eBook Management: Calibre Software

The links above are underlined to show that they are hyperlinks to websites where for the software and products being mentioned. You will see these throughout the book. Some of these products are free, and some are affiliate links to products and software I use and recommend. If you are reading this as a paperback book which you purchased from Amazon and want access to the links, you can download the eBook version of the book for only $2.99 through the Amazon Matchbook program.

WRITE YOUR BOOK

The first step to getting your book published is also the hardest step: Before you can get published, you have to write your book. There are countless thousands of people who want to get published but who never actually write a single page of their book. They want to be authors, but they never author anything. So if you want to set yourself apart from all the other wannabe authors in the world, the first thing to do is to actually become an author. How? Write something!

Now before I am even two paragraphs into this "bare bones basic" book of how to get published, I am already tempted to turn aside and write a moving piece about the hard work of writing, and how writing is 90% perspiration and 10% inspiration, and how you should write for free until someone pays to read, and other such encouraging words. But I will refrain. This is not that kind of book. No inspiration allowed!

I assume that you want to write a book or are in the process of writing one and are looking for a few steps for putting what you write into print. Let me provide a few tips for getting started in writing, and then a few steps for writing in a way that will help prepare your book for publication.

HOW TO GET STARTED IN WRITING

Before you can get published, you must write something. If you already write, skip this section. Otherwise, here are two short tips for getting started as an author.

❑ Write Something Short

One of the things holding potential authors back from writing is the daunting task of writing a full-length novel or non-fiction book. The typical 200-page book contains about 60,000 words, which, if you have never written much of anything before, is *a lot of words!* So start out small. The beauty of eBooks is that they can be any length at all. The first eBook I ever wrote was only about 5,000 words long, but it taught me the process of writing a book and preparing it for publication as an eBook. So if you have never written a book before, you might not want to begin with the million word multi-volume epic. Start with something shorter so you can learn the steps of getting published, and so you can feel the satisfaction of having a book published. This will inspire you to write the second book, and the third.

If 5,000 words even sounds like too much, then start even smaller. Start a blog. In fact, later in this book, I will recommend you start a blog as a way to connect with potential readers, so you might as well do it now. You can start one for free through Blogger.com or Wordpress.com. Begin a habit of writing posts several times a week that are 300-500 words each. But don't think that simply by starting a blog you will instantly gain thousands of readers. You won't. It is quite likely that initially, no one will read your blog. Not even your mother. But remember that the initial goal for writing is not to get readers, but for you to become a better writer. As you write, whether it is blog posts or short eBooks, you will gain confidence as a writer, will develop the habit of writing, build your audience, and may even "find your voice," all of which are crucial for successful authors.

❑ Write for Yourself

Don't write about something you think will "sell." Don't write for your potential audience. Don't write to fix society, correct people, or change the world. These things are a recipe for disaster and frustration.

Just write for yourself. Write to keep yourself entertained, informed, and interested. If you get bored with what you are writing, you will never gain readers because they will be bored too. Write what interests and inspires you, and you will have a better chance of inspiring others.

HOW TO WRITE WITH PUBLICATION IN MIND

The old saying, "An ounce of prevention is worth a pound of cure" is true in writing as well. Write your books the right way the first time, and it will save you hundreds of hours of mind-numbing reformatting down the road.

I am not talking about editing your manuscript. That step will be necessary no matter what. No, I am talking about writing in such so that from the first word of the first paragraph your book is properly formatted for publishing. If you prepare your manuscript properly before you ever even type a single word, it will save you hours of headaches later. To do this, here are the things you need to know:

❑ Write with Styles

This does not refer to your writing style. Hopefully your writing does have its own unique style, but that is not what I am talking about. When I say, "Write with Styles," I mean that when you write, you need to use something in your word processor called "Styles." Every paragraph, every heading, every line needs to use a particular Style. You should never change your font, text size, or paragraph indentation without doing it with Styles.

If you have ever used <u>Microsoft Word</u> (or some of the other popular word processors like <u>WordPerfect</u>, <u>OpenOffice</u>, or <u>Google Docs</u>), you will have seen the Style settings in one of your toolbars, though you may not have ever known what they are for. Typically, they look something like this:

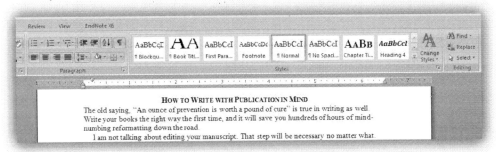

Styles control every element of your manuscript layout, and help make sure that you are maintaining consistency in how your document is laid out. They control which fonts you use, as well as where and how you use them. Styles control the font size of your paragraphs and your headings, and whether your subheadings will use **bold**, *italics,* or SMALL CAPS. Another nice feature of Styles is that if you want to change something throughout your entire document, you can simply change the Style definitions, and every place in the entire document which uses that style will immediately change as well. This will save you a lot of time.

But using Styles doesn't just help you type and format your manuscript. Styles become even more important when you are preparing your manuscript for publication. All eBook formats are based off of the HTML coding language, which is what websites use. Modern HTML also uses something called CSS, or Cascading Style Sheets. Do you see that middle word there? Yes, "style." HTML uses Styles. This means that when you begin to convert your manuscript into an HTML document for an eBook, the Styles in your manuscript can easily and quickly be converted into the Styles for the HTML document. Better yet, if you have used Styles properly, Microsoft Word does the conversion for you. It's as simple as saving your Word document as an HTML document. We will look at this in more detail later.

For now, it is important to know how to use Styles. While you could use the default Styles that are built-in to Microsoft Word, I do not recommend it. Your book will look like Mickey Mouse put it together, with lots of weird colors, underlining, and formatting. To make your book look like an actual book, you will need to create your own Styles. This is not difficult to do, but you need to be aware of all the formatting decisions that go into each and every piece of your book. What should the font be for the paragraphs, headings, and subheadings? How large do you want these fonts, and what special formatting do you want them to have? How much spacing do you want to precede and follow each section? Do you want it left justified, right justified, full justified, or centered?

These are just a few of the decisions that must be asked when you are creating your own Styles.

Though creating Styles sounds like quite a chore, if you get a book out which has formatting you really like, and start measuring the pieces with a ruler, you will find that in just a few minutes, you can pretty much replicate the formatting of that book for your own manuscript. And once this step is done, it's done forever. You can reuse these Styles in every manuscript you ever type by simply saving your document as a Document Template.

In fact, I have a Manuscript Template which you can download for free at the "Manuscript Guidelines" section of RedeemingPress.com. That Manuscript Template not only includes the Styles I usually use in most of my publishing projects, but also includes descriptions of the settings I used for each Style, and some of the other styling decisions and layout options that goes into writing and publishing a book. Even if you don't use the Manuscript Template to write your own books, you might find some of the information helpful. So feel free to go download it and use it "as is" or to change the Styles to whatever you want.

While you are on that page downloading the Template, you might also want to watch the YouTube Video I put there about using Styles in Microsoft Word. It contains some of the information I have included here, but it also shows me actually using the Styles in Microsoft Word to demonstrate what they do and how they work. You can also watch the video here: Use Styles Video.

❏ Use a Style Guide

Along with using Styles, one of the things you will also want to use in typing your manuscript is a Style Guide. Confused? I just finished writing about using Styles in your manuscript, and now I encourage you to use something called a

"Style Guide." Aren't they the same thing? No, they are not. They are very different, and you need both while you are writing your manuscript.

While Styles are a way of formatting the look and feel of your manuscript, a Style Guide helps make sure that your manuscript is consistent in how it treats punctuation, spelling, abbreviation, and capitalization. For example, when you reference a year in your manuscript, are you going to write it 400 BC, 400 B.C., 400 BCE, or 400 B.C.E. Whichever way you choose is fine, but you need to make a decision, and then make sure that whatever way you choose, you follow this method consistently throughout the entire manuscript.

When it comes to Style Guides, hundreds of decisions need to be made about things like whether periods and commas go inside or outside of quote marks, whether to use footnotes, endnotes, or parenthetical notes, how to abbreviate and capitalize a myriad of words, titles, places, and names, and a whole host of other such details. While it may seem that such decisions are insignificant, they can make or break a book.

Thankfully, you don't have to create your own Style Guide from scratch. There are dozens of such Style Guides already available online and in bookstores. For example, the Business Writing blog offers a free <u>Title and Subtitle capitalization guide</u> which helps you figure out which words should be capitalized in your titles and headings. Other websites offer other suggestions and capitalization guides as well, though if you want a comprehensive guide, you will probably have to buy a book. The most popular Style Guide is the *Chicago Manual of Style,* but this volume provides way more information than most writers need. For Christian authors, I recommend *Zondervan's Style Guide*, and *The Little Style Guide*.

Of course, if you don't want to buy a Style Guide, I have also included a short Style Guide as part of the <u>Manuscript Template</u> which I mentioned in the previous section. This basic Style Guide is the one I use for the books I write. Most of my writing is geared toward non-fiction books on Scripture and Theology (though some critics think all my books are fiction), and so a lot of the details in my Style Guide have to do with abbreviations for Bible book names, and common theological or biblical terms. Whether you use this Style Guide or not, it will show you what sorts of things to include in your Style Guide so you can get started on developing your own.

❑ Check for Orphans and Widows

In the Bible, James writes that true religion looks after orphans and widows in their distress. He was not thinking about book publishing when he wrote that, but authors still need to look after orphans and widows in their manuscripts so that they do not cause distress.

First, you need to understand what orphans and widows are. There is actually a bit of disagreement in the typesetting community on what the difference is between an orphan and a widow, but essentially, orphans and widows short lines of text or individual words that stand alone at the end or beginning of a paragraph, or at the end or beginning of a column. Here is an image which helps clarify how orphans and widows appear in your manuscript.

Nunc viverra imperdiet enim. Fusce est. Vivamus a tellus.

Lorem ipsum dolor sit amet, consectetuer adipiscing elit. Maecenas porttitor congue massa. Fusce posuere, magna sed pulvinar ultricies, purus lectus malesuada libero, sit amet commodo magna eros quis urna.

Aenean nec lorem. In porttitor. Fusce posuere, magna sed pulvinar Donec laoreet nonummy augue.

Suspendisse dui purus, scelerisque at, vulputate vitae, pretium mattis, nunc. Mauris eget neque at sem venenatis eleifend. Ut nonummy.

Fusce aliquet pede non pede. Suspendisse

dapibus lorem pellentesque magna.

Donec blandit feugiat ligula. Donec hendrerit, felis et imperdiet euismod, purus ipsum pretium metus, in lacinia nulla nisl eget sapien. Donec ut est in lectus consequat consequat.

Etiam eget dui. Aliquam erat volutpat. Sed at lorem in nunc porta tristique.

Proin nec augue. Quisque aliquam tempor magna. Pellentesque habitant morbi tristique senectus et netus et malesuada fames ac turpis egestas.

Nunc ac magna. Maecenas odio dolor, vulputate vel, auctor ac, accumsan id, felis. Pellentesque cursus sagittis felis.

Essentially, what you don't want is words all by themselves at the end of a paragraph, as you see two examples of this above. Also, you do not want a single line of a paragraph all by itself at either the top or the bottom of a page or column. The image above has an example of each.

There are two ways of fixing orphan and widow errors in your manuscript. You can fix all these manually by adding or deleting words to paragraphs until the orphans and widows are corrected, or you can allow Microsoft Word to do the work for you

There are two ways of fixing orphan and widow errors in your manuscript. You can fix all these manually by adding or deleting words to paragraphs until the orphans and widows are corrected, or you can allow Microsoft Word to do the work for you.

To allow Microsoft Word to check for orphans and widows, go the paragraph options of Word, and click the "Line and Page Breaks" tab. Check the "Widow/ Orphan Control" box and click "OK" at the bottom. Microsoft Word will correct most of the orphans and widows in your manuscript.

For some reason, Microsoft Word does not find and correct all of these orphans and widows in your manuscript, and so you can either call it "good enough" or manually fix the few that do not get corrected as you type.

USING IMAGES IN YOUR BOOK

Using images in your book adds an entirely new dimension to your writing. But images also add an increased level of difficulty. Therefore, I highly recommend that first-time publishers avoid using images in their book if at all possible. Learn the process of publishing an imageless book before tackling the numerous problems that arise when trying to insert images into your book.

However, if you feel fairly confident of your ability to publish a book according to the steps laid out in this guide so far, or if you absolutely *must* include images in your book, then some of the tips and suggestions on the following pages will help.

❑ Find and Save Your Images

The first step, of course, is to find the images you want to include in your book, and then save them somewhere on your computer. If you are taking images off your camera or using some sort of digital software to create your images, hopefully you know the steps involved to saving your files in a particular location. If you are going to use images from the internet, you need to make sure that you purchase the images you are going to use, or make sure that the images you use are not under Copyright and are royalty-free.

I often search the following websites for images. Not all of these are free, but they do tell you which ones are free, which ones you must pay for, and if you buy them, what printing and publishing rights come with the images.

- SXC.hu – This is a Stock Photo Exchange website. It is one of my favorite sites, as it has one of the largest selections of free stock photos. For most images, all you need to do is give credit to the photographer in your published work, but make sure you read the rights for an image before using it.

- Search.CreativeComons.org – This is my second favorite site for free stock photos. These images are usually web-based images that are pulled from websites that have agreed to fall under the Creative Commons publishing license. As with SXC.hu, make sure you read the publishing rights before using an image from this site.
- iStockPhoto.com – iStock Photo has a large selection of images, but most are not free. However, you might notice upon visiting their website that they announce "royalty-free" images. Most of the following websites will state the same thing, so it is important to understand the distinction. A free image, obviously, is completely free. But then there are royalty-free images. You have to make a one-time purchase of these images, but once purchased, you do not need to make ongoing royalty payments based on how many times the image is used or printed. Images that require royalties also require that you make ongoing payments based on number of books sold, or number of locations the image is used. I strongly recommend that you stay away from images that require royalties.
- GettyImages.com – Getty Images is one of the leaders in the online photo industry, and has a large variety of high quality images.
- Deviantart.com – The images at Deviant Art are not for the timid. These are creative and odd images, sometimes bordering on scandalous. But if you are looking for an eye-popping, attention-grabbing image, this website is the place to start.
- DreamsTime.com – This is another great collection of photos and stock images. Like many of the other sites, they also have a large number of free images.
- ShutterStock.com – Shutter Stock offers a huge selection of images and art. As with the other sites, many are royalty-free.
- Photos.com – What can I say? Just like the other sites, a large number of images are available, and most are royalty-free.
- DepositPhotos.com – Okay, it's getting old to keep saying it, so this will be the last time. This site has millions of images, and most are royalty-free.

❑ **Compress Your Images**

Many publishing websites have limits to the size of the document that can be uploaded for publication. For example, Smashwords has a 10 MB file size limit and Amazon's limit currently sits at 50 MB. Adding images to your book will greatly increase the file size of your book, and you also need to save room for the cover image.

So after you find the images you are going to insert into your book, you need to compress them so they maintain their quality but take up as little memory as possible. One of the best ways of doing this is by using photo-editing software like Adobe Photoshop, or a free online application like Google's Picasa. I will not provide tutorials on how to use these programs to compress your images, but the basic goals are to reduce the dimensions of the images to the actual dimensions you will use in your book and to reduce the dpi (dots per inch) of your images to around 300 dpi or so for a paperback, and 96 dpi for an eBook.

However, while such photo-editing software is the best way to compress your images, Microsoft Word has decent photo-editing capabilities built right in. For this book, I will show you how to use these tools. On this current book I was able to achieve a 60% reduction in the file size for my book simply by using the Microsoft Word image compression feature.

❏ **Insert Your Images**

To edit and compress your images, you first need to insert them into your document. To insert an image, go to the "Insert" tab of your menu bar, select "Picture" and then go to the file on your computer where you saved your images. Find the image you want to use, select it, and then click "Insert." The image will get inserted into your document.

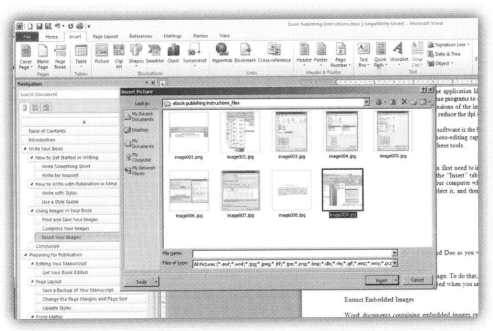

❏ **Edit Your Images in Microsoft Word**

Once your image is inserted, there are a few things you want to do to the image so that it takes up as little memory as possible, and so that it displays properly in both the paperback and eBook editions of your book. If you already compressed your images using a photo-editing program as suggested above, you may still want to follow the compression techniques suggested here to make sure your images are optimized for use in Microsoft Word.

To compress and edit an image in your manuscript, begin by clicking on the image itself. When you do, the "Picture Tools" tab becomes available on your menu bar. But before you go click on that tab, center your image on your page by clicking the "Center" button or selecting the "Centered Normal" style.

After you have centered your image, go click on the "Picture Tools" tab, and look to the far right where you have some photo editing tools such as Position, Wrap Text, Crop, Height, and Width. Make sure that the Position and Wrap Text are set to "In line with Text." While other settings are possible, this setting is the easiest one to get working with the lay-out requirements for the Kindle, Nook, and iPad. If you need to crop or resize your images, feel free to do that as well using the appropriate buttons and settings on the right of the menu bar. Make sure that your images are as large as possible, but not larger than the width of your text, and especially not larger than the rec-

Make sure that your images are as large as possible, but not larger than the width of your text, and especially not larger than the recommended image size limit for the Kindle, Nook, and iPad.

ommended image size limit for the Kindle, Nook, and iPad. I recommend your interior images be no wider than 5 inches, and no taller than 6.9 inches.

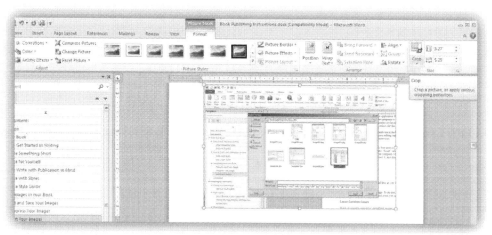

To add some picture styles such as a drop shadow or border outline, use the buttons and options in the center of the menu bar. For the images in this book, I used the "Center Shadow Rectangle" preset.

Finally, you should compress your images using the "Compress Pictures" button. I recommend using the default settings, which compresses only the image you are currently working on, deletes all the cropped parts of the image, and saves the image at 200 dpi.

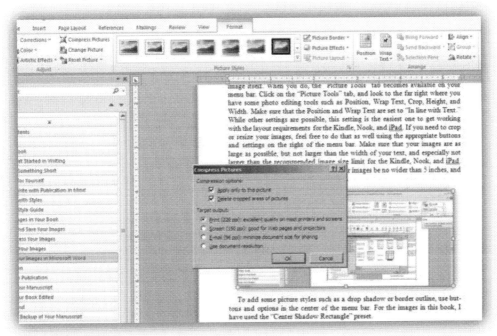

If you end up with a manuscript file that is too large, you can come back and reduce all images down to 150 dpi to see if that reduces your file size to within the size limits. If not, you can try the 96 dpi option, but that is not recommended, as your images might start looking grainy and distorted in your paperback editions of the book and some eReader screens.

One final thing to check is that your images are not "scaled down." Not only can this cause problems with the appearance and layout of the image in the eBook versions of your book, but having a scaled down image means that the actual image size is larger than what is being shown, which means it is taking up more memory than necessary. The way to fix this is to go the far right of the "Picture Tools" menu, and click the little drop-down arrow button in the "Size" section so that the "Advanced Layout: Size" options appear.

If you end up with a manuscript file that is too large, you can come back and reduce all images down to 150 dpi to see if that reduces your file size to within the size limits.

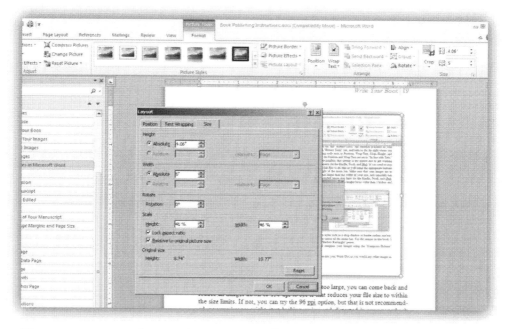

If you compressed your image according to the previous paragraph, the "Scale" section should say 100% in both width and height. If it doesn't say this, you will need to compress the image again, or change a few of the other settings so that the image which is being shown on your page is being shown at 100% the height and width of the actual image. You do not want scaling of images.

That is about it for inserting and editing images within your manuscript. You will learn in the chapter on Formatting the eBook on how to extract your embedded images into a folder for the HTML file you will be creating, but you don't need to learn about that now.

CONCLUSION

This is all I am going to say about how to write your manuscript. As you can see, writing a manuscript is about way more than just getting some words onto a page. While most writers and authors do not like to concern themselves with the little details about how to prepare the manuscript for publication, taking care of these little details at the beginning of your writing process will save you scores of hours later as you try to format your manuscript to make it look like an actual eBook or paperback book.

Of course, even if you are pursuing the traditional publishing route, it is still wise to write your manuscript using Styles and a Style Guide. Most traditional publishing companies do not expect authors to submit manuscripts that are perfectly in line with the company's typesetting Styles or in-house Style Guide. In fact, no matter how you prepare your manuscript for submission, they have teams of editors who will bring your manuscript in line with their in-house rules anyway.

If this is the case, why write your manuscript using Styles and a Style Guide? For two reasons. First, it will still set your manuscript apart from other manuscripts if yours looks more professional and polished. Using Styles and a Style Guide makes it look like you actually know what you are doing. Second, if by some chance you are not able to get your manuscript published using traditional routes and you decide to publish your book on your own or through a publishing company like Redeeming Press, you do not have to pour hundreds of hours into properly preparing and proof-reading your manuscript for publication. If you typed it right the first time, the book is immediately ready to enter the editorial and typesetting stages.

With that in mind, let us move on to the steps we follow at Redeeming Press to turn manuscripts into books.

PREPARE FOR PUBLICATION

Once your manuscript is finished and has been typed according to your satisfaction, there are still several steps that need to be done before you are ready for publication. These steps are listed below.

EDITING YOUR MANUSCRIPT

The first thing you need to do is get your manuscript edited. While you may think that your manuscript is error free and is perfect just as you wrote it, the fact of the matter is that you probably have several typographical and grammatical errors on every page, and it is quite likely that several sections of the book are unclear and poorly written. An editor will help you find and fix these areas.

If you don't know an editor, just do a Google search for editors, or check out some of the people who are offering their services on Elance.com. Of course, editing can get quite expensive. Editors will charge about $30 per hour or $3 per page. If you hire an editor, make sure you send them your Style Guide so that they can compare it with your manuscript as they work through it.

However, most new authors cannot afford to pay an editor. If that is your situation, you should at least try to find several people who will be willing to proofread your manuscript for typographical errors. You might have some family members or friends who will do this for free. For myself, my wife reads everything I write, and she does a good job finding numerous mistakes. I am also part of a small group of authors who work together to proofread and edit each other's books.

The bottom line when it comes to editing and proofreading your manuscript is that the more eyes that look at your manuscript, the better your manuscript will be.

PAGE LAYOUT

Once the manuscript is typed and edited, you are ready to begin preparing your manuscript for publication. This is done by taking your finished manuscript and formatting it to look like the pages of a book. This is done using the following steps.

❏ Save a Backup of Your Manuscript

Formatting your document to look like a book can mess up the manuscript pretty quickly, so save yourself some potential headaches in the future, and save a backup copy of your finished manuscript.

❏ Change the Page Margins and Page Size

If you used a Manuscript Template like the one I told you about the previous chapter, your page sizes are 8.5 x 11 inches, the size of a normal sheet of paper. Very few books are printed on this size of paper, and so you need to adjust your page size to match that of a book.

In Microsoft Word, this is done by going to "Page Layout" and selecting "Margins." In the drop-down menu, select "Custom Margins."

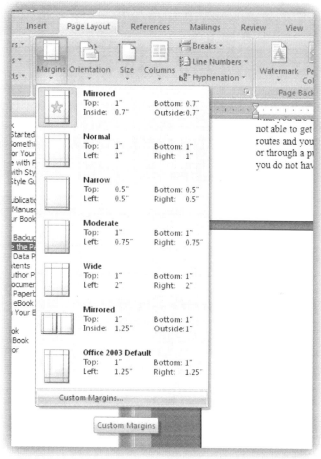

A separate window will open with three tabs up top: Margins, Paper, and Layout. Changes will be made in all three tabs.

Start first with the "Margins" tab, which should be the tab that is already selected. Enter margin sizes of 1 inch on the top, 0.7 on the bottom, left, and right, and use a Gutter of 0.2 inches. The gutter allows for a little extra space for the inner margin of the book where the pages attach to the spine. Also make sure you select the "Mirror Margins" option under pages.

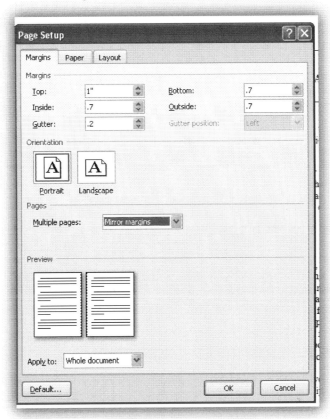

Now go over to the "Paper" tab. In the options that are shown there, make your paper width and height match that of popular paperback book sizes, and also change the margins to match that of a typical book as well. While there are a variety of paperback book sizes, the most popular size is 5.5 x 8.5 inches. However, various types of books call for various types of page sizes. Since this current book is a "how-to" book with images, I am going to make the book a little larger than I would if I was writing one of my books on theology. Whatever page size you set your book to, you will want to make sure you keep them within the standard publishing trim sizes (5.25x8, 5.5x8.5, 6x9, 7x10, 8x10, 8.25x6, 8.25x8.25).

Make your paper width and height match that of popular paperback book sizes, and also change the margins to match that of a typical book as well.

Pick a book trim size that fits your book type, and set these as described above. Make sure you apply these settings to the whole document.

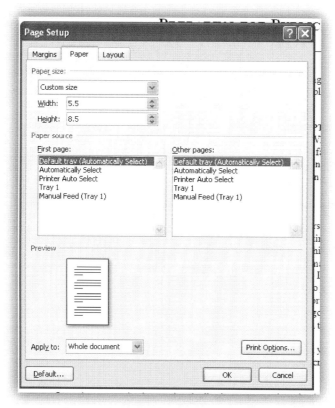

Finally, change the footer size and layout options so that they match what is normally found in a book. This is done in the same window that has the "Paper" and "Margins" tabs, but select the "Layout" tab instead. First, select the options for "Different Odd and Even Pages" and for "Different First Page." Then enter a header margin of 0.5 inches and a footer margin of 0.0 inches.

> *Change the footer size and layout options so that they match what is normally found in a book.*

If you are going to use footnotes on your pages, you may want to choose a different footer margin size. Of course, with most publishing programs like Microsoft Word, choosing a larger footer margin simply means that there will be more white space beneath the footnotes that get entered. Typically, if you are using footnotes, the word processing program will adjust the text height and footer area according to how many footnotes need to fit on the page. The footer margin will get added to the bottom of these footnotes. However, you will need to play around with these settings a bit and adjust them to whatever you think is best for your particular book setting and layout. My preferred layout setting, however, is to leave the footer margin at 0.0 inches.

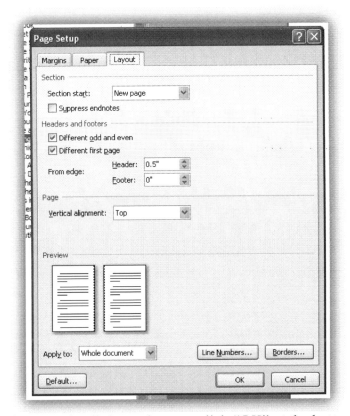

When you have made all these changes, click "OK" at the bottom of the window, and your entire document will reformat to look more like the pages of a book. But you are not done yet!

❑ **Update Styles**

You may have noticed that as a result of changing your paper size and margins, some of the Styles in your manuscript got messed up a little bit. For example, your chapter titles might look a little scrunched.

Also, you may note that while most published books have their paragraph text left and right justified, your manuscript is only left justified. It is time to fix all these issues, and a few others.

This is an example of a place where using Styles from the very beginning will save you a lot of time. If you used Styles, all you have to do is go edit the Styles, and the entire manuscript will change to reflect the new rules. But if you didn't use Styles, then you are going to waste a few hours going through your entire document and updating, fixing, and correcting every paragraph, every title, and every subtitle, one by one.

For most of my books, I edit the Chapter Title Style so that the left and right indentation is smaller, somewhere between .2 and .5 inches on the left and right.

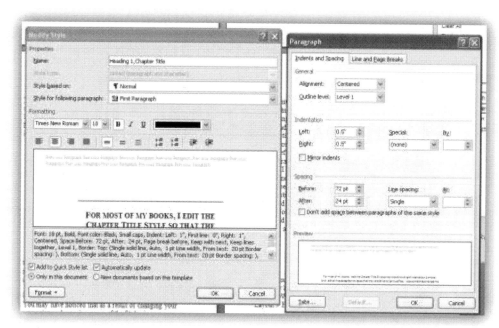

I also edit all the paragraph styles so that they are left and right justified, and sometimes I change the fonts throughout the document to something more professional looking, like Adobe Garamond Pro (A premium font I purchased from Adobe). I usually set the chapter titles to "Adobe Garamond Pro Bold 18 point" font, and the paragraph Styles (Normal Paragraph and First Paragraph) to "Adobe Garamond Pro 12 point" font. But you can use whatever you fonts and settings look the best to you.

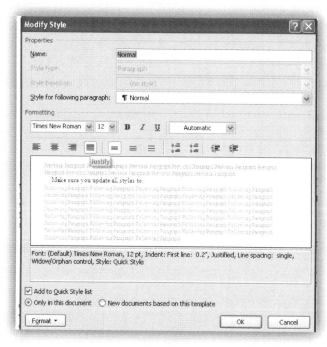

One final thing I do to the layout is to allow hyphenation throughout the document. Fully justified paragraphs sometimes do strange things to the spacing of the words. In fact, without hyphenation, the first line of this very paragraph looks rather odd:

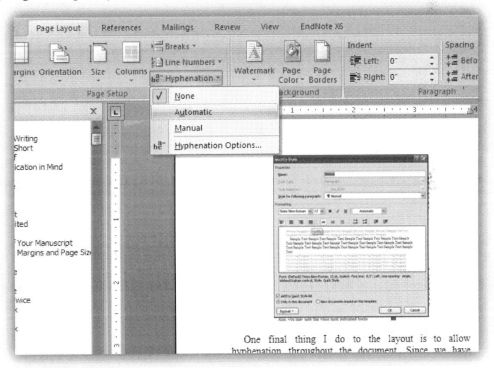

Once I turn on hyphenation, it allows the program to cut words at syllable breaks so that the paragraph text is evenly spaced. You turn on hyphenation by going to "Page Layout," selecting "Hyphenation" and setting it to "Automatic."

You may be noticing that while your book is starting to look more like an actual book, it is missing some main sections, such as the Title Page, Bibliographic Page, and the Table of Contents. So let's add these first pages now.

FRONT MATTER

There are numerous front matter pages that can be added to your document, but you really only need to focus on the three most common, the Title Page, the Bibliographic Page, and the Table of Contents.

❏ Insert a Title Page

Now that you have the page layout set up, it is time to start making your book look more like an actual book. This involves starting at the beginning and adding the various elements of a book that might be missing. You can pick up almost any book on your shelf and start flipping through it to see what elements are missing from your book.

The first obvious missing element is the Title Page. This is simply a page in your book which contains nothing but your book title, your name as the author, and the publisher's name at the bottom. Frequently there are two versions of the Title Page, one with just the book title, followed by a second page with the author's name and publisher's information. I will show you how to add both pages, and if you want to delete the first page for your eBook, you can easily do so.

To begin, just go to the top of the first page of your book, and insert a page. But do not insert the page by clicking "Insert" and "Blank Page." What you want is not just a new page, but a new section as well. I will explain why later when you insert page numbers and header titles. To insert both a blank page *and* a new document section, go to "Page Layout" and click the "Breaks" button, and under "Section Breaks" select "Next Page."

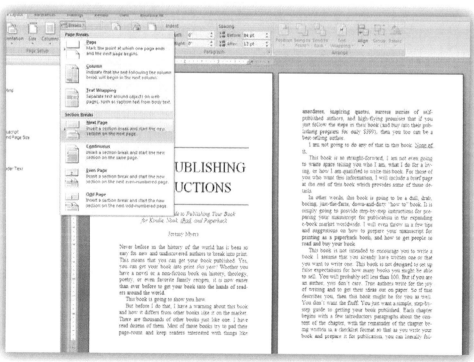

Take note of the steps you use to add this new page and new section, because you will be using it frequently in later steps. Rather than show the image on how to insert a new section page each time, I will simply instruct you to "insert a new section page."

So now that you have your new first page, you can add the Title of the book to this page. Go ahead and use the Book Title Style for the Title Page.

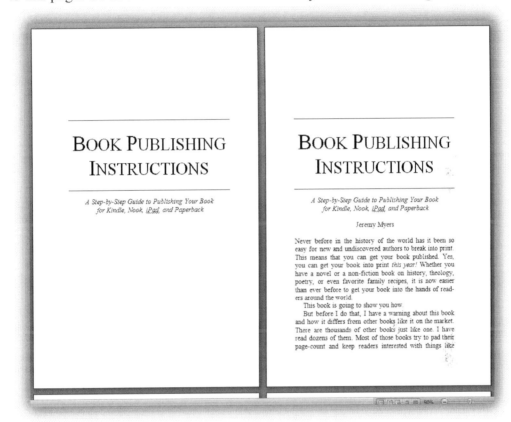

Now you are going to follow all these steps *again* to create your second Title Page, but this one will include the author's name somewhere near the middle, and the publisher's name near the bottom. Note that in the image above, I already have part of this second Title Page showing there, and the paragraph text is part of the Preface to this book.

Note also that in between the two Title Pages you need a blank page. If you look at books which have these two title pages, the first Title Page is on the right-hand side of the open book, and when you turn the page, there is a blank page on the left, and the second Title Page is on the right. You can duplicate this layout by inserting a new section page twice (so that you now have three in a row) and putting your second Title page on the third new section page. You should also "insert a new section page" at the beginning of the book preface so that it also begins on its own page and with its own section. All of these new sections will become very important later when you add page numbers and header titles to the book.

So for now, your manuscript should look something like this (I have zoomed out on the four opening pages so you can see it a little better):

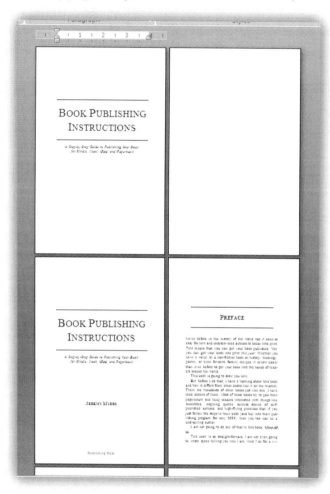

In case you didn't catch it in the image above, I not only added some styling to my name as the author, but I also added the "Redeeming Press" name to the footer of the second Title Page. I will add further details to Publisher name later, but have typed it in now to serve as a placeholder.

You may also note in the image above that I created a "Preface" chapter title using the Chapter Title Style. However, in a normal book, what usually follows the second Title Page? It is not the Preface, but a page of tiny print which includes all the Bibliographic data for the book. So let us add one of those next.

❑ Bibliographic Data Page

Once again, insert a new section page for the Bibliographic Page. What goes on this page depends on how much data you have. At the bare minimum, you want to include all the data that a person would need for a footnote entry or bibliography in the back of a book or term paper. This includes the title of the book, the author, the publisher, the city and state of the publisher, and the year the book was published. Look in some of your favorite books for how this information is formatted and choose a format that looks best to you.

Other than the details listed above, you will also want to include some additional information if it is available for your book, or if it is required by law.

For example, many books include Library of Congress Cataloguing in Publication Data. You can learn more about these details at www.loc.gov, but the process to obtain this information is somewhat involved, and if you are self-publishing your book, the Library of Congress will not give it to you anyway. They only provide this information to established publishing companies which publish a certain number of books per year from various authors. So don't worry about including these details in your book.

One thing you will definitely want to include is an ISBN number. Though many self-published authors think they do not need an ISBN number, they are required if you are going to publish your book with Apple iBooks. There are a couple ways of obtaining one. If you publish your book on Smashwords, they can provide you with an ISBN, or you can get one through CreateSpace publishing for a small fee. However, the drawback to both of these options is that the listed publisher for these ISBN numbers will be the company that gave them to you, either Smashwords or CreateSpace. To have yourself listed as the publisher, you will need to obtain your own ISBN number.

To get you own ISBN number, you purchase them from Bowker ISBN service at www.myidentifiers.com. But be warned! If you are buying just one or two, they are not cheap. A single ISBN costs $125. The more you buy, the cheaper they get. So, for example, if you are need two, you might as well buy ten, because either way, the cost is $250. And if you think you need three or four, you might as well buy 100 for $575.

But it gets even worse. Each unique format of your book requires its own ISBN number, and future editions of your book require a new ISBN number. So, for example, every time I publish a book, I use up at least three ISBN numbers. I use one for the paperback edition, one of the Kindle edition (.mobi format), and one for the iPad and Nook edition (ePub format). Technically, I should use a fourth for the Adobe PDF edition, but I figure that the PDF book format is identical to the paperback format, and so I save an ISBN number by combining those two formats.

Whatever ISBN numbers you use, they should also be included in the Bibliography page. I put all the numbers together like this:

ISBN: 978-0-123456-47-1 (Paper)
ISBN: 978-0-123456-47-2 (Mobi)
ISBN: 978-0-123456-47-3 (ePub)

The modern publishing standard is to use the ISBN-13 number. If you obtain the shorter ISBN-10 number somehow, you do not need to include it. Instead, go to a site like www.isbn-13.info to convert the ISBN-10 to an ISBN-13.

One final note about ISBN numbers is that if you purchase your own from Bowker Identifier Services, once you assign the number to a book, you need to enter this identification into their website database through the "Manage ISBNS" section of the website: www.myidentifiers.com/manage_isbns.

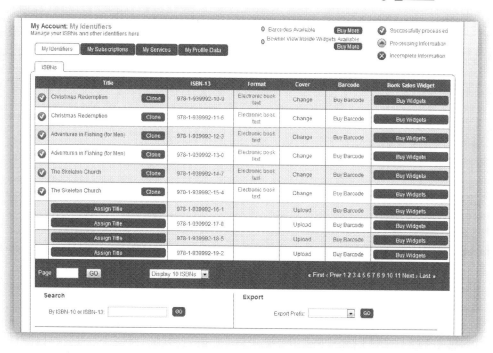

I am not going to walk you through this process, as it is pretty self-explanatory. All you need to do is enter as many details about the book as possible. Again, you don't have to do any of this if your use a Smashwords or CreateSpace ISBN number.

A fourth element you may want to include on your Bibliography page is a copyright permission. This is not necessary to maintain your copyright under the Copyright Law, but it never hurts to include legal statements.

On a related note, if you are writing a book which quotes or references the Bible, the Bibliographic page must include permission statements from every Bible translation you quote from. You can obtain these permission statements from the Bible Translation publisher's website, or simply from the bibliography pages of other books. If there is a primary translation used in the book, note that as well by saying, "Unless otherwise noted, all Scripture quotations are taken from the New King James Version." Obviously, substitute in your preferred Bible translation.

When you are done, you Bibliography page may look something like this:

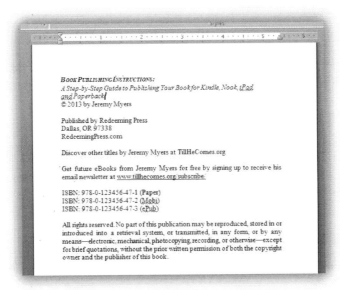

❑ Dedication Page

Following the Bibliography page, a reader usually encounters a Dedication page. Most often, this page is completely blank with just a line or two dedicating the book to a person or group of people who encouraged the author to write, or were influential in the creation and publication of this book. Occasionally, the Dedication page is either replaced or followed by a "With Special Thanks" page which contains several paragraphs on how the book came into existence and lists several people who helped move the book toward publication. Include whatever you think is best. For this book, I am dedicating it to my wife, who reads everything I write and is my number one fan.

To create the Dedication page, you will once again insert a new section page, and then type in whatever you want on that page. Though it may change some before this book goes into print, here is an image of my Dedication page:

For my wife, Wendy.

Thanks for reading everything I write—no matter how boring, and through it all, remaining my number one fan.

❏ Table of Contents

The Table of Contents usually follows the Dedication page. Inserting a Table of Contents is usually one of the last things you want to do for your book, but Microsoft Word makes it relatively easy to update your Table of Contents later if you change your pagination. So while my book is not close to done at the time I am inserting my Table of Contents, I will insert it now, and then update it when my book is finished.

To insert the Table of Contents, you will insert a new section page, and then click on the "References" tab in the menu bar and click "Table of Contents." From the drop-down menu, select the "Insert Table of Contents" option near the bottom of the menu. The reason you should select this option is because you want to choose the formatting and depth for your Table of Contents.

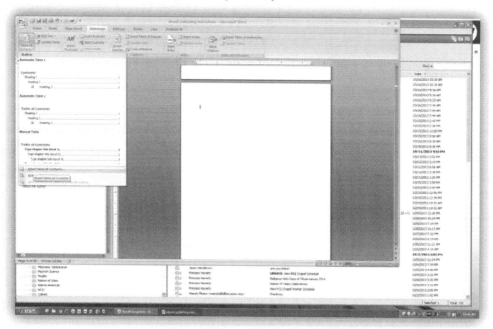

When choosing how many levels deep your Table of Contents will go, I recommend that if your book is long, just go with one level deep, as this will include only your chapter titles. But if your book is short or if you want a long and detailed Table of Contents, feel free to have the Table go two or three levels deep.

Since this current book is more of a reference guide for publishing books, I want a long and detailed Table of Contents so people can quickly and easily find the page they are looking for. So for that, I am going to create a Table of Contents that is three levels deep. This will include the chapter title, the sub-section titles, and the various steps for each section.

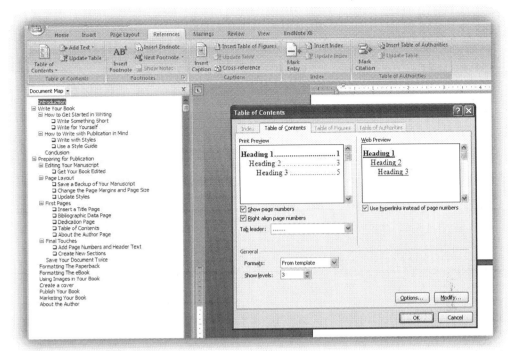

You can see that I allow the dotted Tab Leader on the Printed pages, but only want Hyperlinks for the Web pages. This will be important later when you prepare your book for eBook publication.

Also, I used the "Modify" button on the lower right to make each level of the Table of Contents look a certain way. If you have toyed around already with creating or modifying your Styles (see Chapter 1), then you already know how to modify the appearance and behavior of the various levels of your Table of Contents. Essentially, all three levels are based on the "First Paragraph" Style. I put the chapter titles in bold, with a 6 point space above, and each subheading of the Table is indented .17 inches, with no additional spacing above or below. If you insert your Table of Contents, and the spacing or styling looks strange, you can modify the table by using this "Modify" button until the Table of Contents looks the way you want it.

If you insert your Table of Contents, and the spacing or styling looks strange, you can modify the table by using the "Modify" button until the Table of Contents looks the way you want it.

Here is how mine currently looks, though the final appearance will be much different.

If you add pages to your book or change the page layout, or do any sort of modifications to your book whatsoever, one thing you will want to do before publishing is update your Table of Contents. This is done by going to the "References" tab in your menu, and then simply clicking "Update Table." It will make sure all the page numbers, chapter titles, and subheadings match what is actually in your book. A window will open which asks if you want to update the page numbers only, or update the entire Table. Choose the second option if you have made changes to chapter titles or subheadings. Otherwise, only updating the page numbers should be sufficient.

Try as you might, the formatting and page numbers of your book will be constantly changing until right before you go to press. So even though you are inserting your Table of Contents now, make sure that one of the last

Make sure that one of the last steps you do before going to press is to return to your Table of Contents and update the page numbers and chapter titles to reflect what is actually in your book.

steps you do before going to press is to return to your Table of Contents and update the page numbers and chapter titles to reflect what is actually in your book.

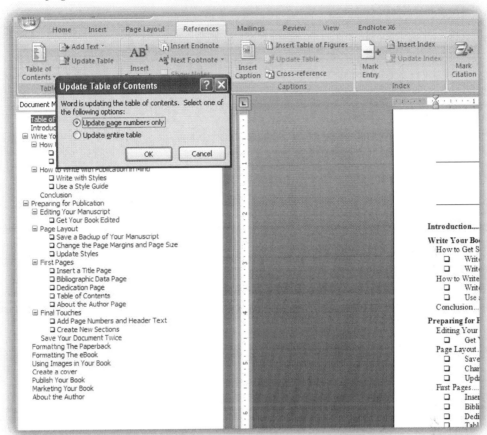

❏ **About the Author Page**

Some authors want to include an "About the Author Page" in their book. If you have other published books, a website, or you like to interact with readers through Facebook or Twitter, adding this page is a good idea. It usually goes at the end of your book. So although I am writing about adding "Front Matter" to your book, I am going to put this "About the Author" page here as well, since you might as well add it in this stage of preparing your book for publication.

Essentially, all you do is go to the last page of your book and insert a new section page. Then type in whatever it is you want your readers to know about you. Write about yourself, your education, your published works, your websites and social sites, and anything else you think is pertinent.

Below is a screenshot of my current Author Page, though it may change by the time this book goes to Publication.

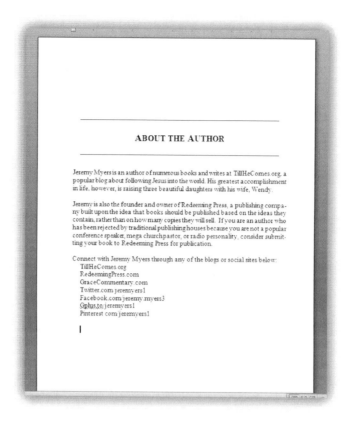

FINAL TOUCHES

You may have noticed that a few major elements are missing from all the pages in your book. Specifically, you are missing page numbers and header titles. You should wait to add these until now so that all the pages throughout the entire manuscript that require page numbers are present. There is no point adding page number before all the pages are inserted. While you can still add pages to the document after the page numbers have been inserted, doing so can sometimes create problems. But now that all the pages are present, you are now ready to add the page numbers and header text.

❏ Create New Sections

The very first step is to make sure that every single new chapter begins a new formatting section in your book. Since you will want to include chapter titles on the top of your odd-numbered (right-hand) pages in your book, each chapter needs to be in its own manuscript section. Thankfully, Microsoft Word has an easy way of doing this. First, it will be helpful to show the "Section" count in the lower left-hand side of your Word window, in the area called the "Status Bar." The default setting here is usually only page count and word count.

If you right-click with your mouse on the Status Bar, you can select which details to show. Select "Sections" to show which section you are in.

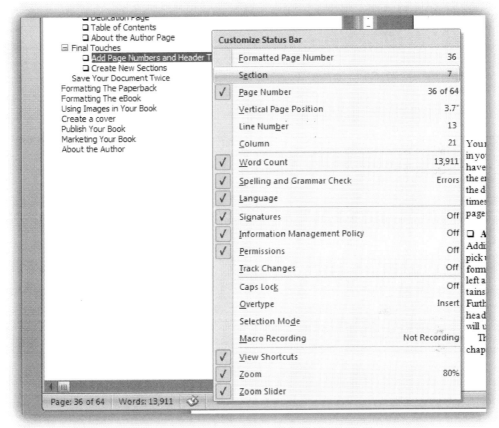

The Status Bar should now show which section you are working in.

If you followed the steps earlier in this chapter of inserting new section pages for each of the "Front Matter" pages of your book, you should already have several "Sections" for your book. You now want to add section breaks to the rest of the book so that each chapter is in its own section. Again, the reason you should do this is so that each chapter can have the chapter title listed at the top of each right-hand page (The book title will go on the top of the left-hand page).

To create a section break at the beginning of each chapter, first click your mouse on the bottom of the page *right before* each new chapter. Then, create a new section page just as you have already done numerous times for your book.

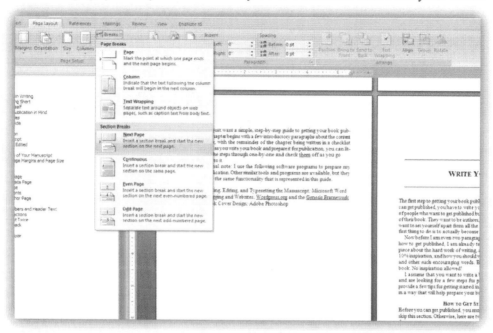

Sometimes adding a new section page like this will also add a blank page to your book. While you *might* want blank pages in between chapters (more on that in the next few paragraphs), right now you do not want a blank page. So if this step adds a blank page to your manuscript, just hit the "Delete" button once on your keyboard, and the chapter should come back up. If you do this, just make sure you didn't accidentally delete the newly-created section break. How can you check? By looking at the section number down on your Status Bar. Click on the last paragraph of the page before the chapter break, and note the section number. Then click on the first paragraph of the new chapter, and make sure the section number is not the same. If it changes, your section break at the new chapter is still intact.

Before you go do this for the next chapter, you want to check one more thing with the chapter you are working on. You need to make sure that each new chapter begins on an odd-numbered page. While this practice is not universally followed in the publishing industry, it is fairly standard. Most of the time, the first page of a new chapter begins on an odd-numbered page, which is a right-hand page. Flip through a few books you have lying around to see if they follow this standard or not. Most professionally-published books will follow this rule. While a chapter might *end* on a left-handed, even-numbered page, it should not start there. So if a chapter ends on a right-handed, odd-numbered page, you need to insert a blank page before the first page of the chapter so that it can begin on the right. Note also that these blank pages before new chapters are always completely blank. They should have no page numbers and no header text. If you see a blank page with page numbers and header text, this is a typesetting mistake by the publisher.

So after you completed the previous step of creating a new page section break at the beginning of each chapter, the next thing to check is to make sure that the page number for that first page of the chapter is an odd number. You can check this down in the Status Bar, right next to the section number. If your cursor is on the first page of a chapter, and the page number is even, you will need to add *an additional* page section break before the chapter. You do not simply want to add a blank page at the end of the previous chapter, because then it will have the page number and header text that you will set up in the next step. You need a completely new section for this page so that it can be completely blank.

To add this blank new section, page, just go to the end of the last page of the previous chapter, and once again, insert a new section page. To verify that this was done correctly, make sure that the end of one chapter is in one section (e.g., Section 7), the blank page is in a second section (e.g., Section 8), and the first page of the next chapter is in a third section (e.g., Section 9). Once this is done, go and repeat these steps for every single chapter in your book.

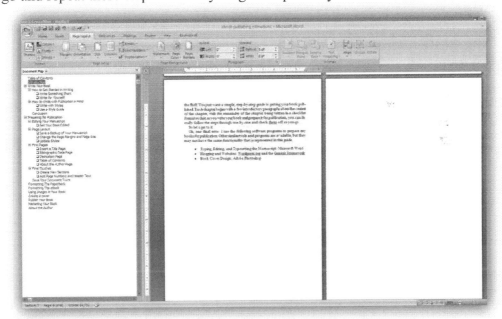

Note that if you view the document in a side-by-side manner as I am doing in the image above, the page layout is actually "reversed." The odd pages are on the left, though in your printed book, they will actually be on the right, and vice versa. So if you view your document in this way, don't let that confuse you! Pay attention to the page number down on the Status Bar, and you will not be deceived by the way the layout looks on your screen.

One other thing to note is that after this point, if you ever make content or style changes to your book, these changes will have a domino effect to your layout. If you add or delete content, this will most likely affect your page count, which will in turn affect whether your chapters begin on odd or even page numbers, which affects whether a blank page should precede the chapter or not. So if you make major changes to your manuscript after this, you must always recheck all the section breaks. It is best, therefore, to make sure your manuscript is complete before doing any of these page break steps.

❏ **Add Page Numbers and Header Text**

After you have added proper section breaks to every chapter in your book, you are now ready to add page numbers and header text to your pages.

But be warned: Adding page numbers and header text to your book can get rather tricky. If you pick up a typical book and look at how the page numbers and header titles are formatted, you will notice that in most books, the page numbers are in the upper left and upper right corners of facing pages, and the header text on the left contains the book title while the header text on the right contains the chapter title. Furthermore, if you look at the very first page of the chapter, there should be no header text or header page numbers at all. If the first page has a page numbers, it will usually be centered in the footer.

There are, of course, alternative locations for page numbers, book titles, and chapter titles, and you can adjust their locations to suit your needs and creativity, but the process I describe below will follow the "normal" pattern that is found in many books.

Begin by double-clicking your mouse in the header section of any page *that is not a first page of a chapter or section*. In other words, since the first page of a chapter should not have page numbers or heading text in the header, do not double-click in the header of the first page of a chapter. Instead, double-click in the header of a second or third page of a chapter. Once you do, it will look like this:

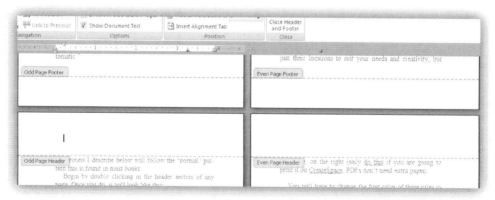

Note that the header sections have a little tab underneath which say "Odd Page Header" or "Even Page Header." It is essential that your headers say this. If they do not, then you have not properly formatted your pages, and need to go back and review the "Change the Page Margins and Paper Size" section earlier in this chapter. You absolutely need different odd and even pages to properly format page numbers and page headers.

Before you insert the page numbers and header text, there is one other critical thing to note, which was hinted at previously. If you inspect the page layout on a typical book, you will see that odd-numbered pages are always on the right, and even-numbered pages are always on the left. If you are holding a book which has this reversed, the typesetter for that book did not know what they were doing. Now look at your computer screen. If you show two pages next to each other as I am doing for the images in this book, the "Odd Page Header" is on the left and the "Even Page Header" is on the right. When inserting page numbers and page

> *Odd-numbered pages are always on the right, and even-numbered pages are always on the left.*

headers, it is an easy mistake to think that because a page is on the left on your screen, it will be on the left in your book. If you make that mistake, when you get your proof back from the printer, you will be shocked to discover that all your page numbers and header titles are not on the outer margins of the page where they should be, but are on the inside, toward the gutter of the page. So pay attention to where you are putting page numbers and header text. No matter how the pages appear on your screen, even-numbered pages are printed on the left and odd-numbered pages are printed on the right. This means that even pages will have their page numbers and header text on the left, and odd pages should have their page numbers and header text on the right. This is why some people just center all the page numbers in the footer, and center all the chapter titles in header. That would make it a bit simpler, but not nearly as professional looking.

So before you start inserting page numbers and header text, make sure you know whether you are inserting "Odd Page Header" numbers and text or "Even Page Header" numbers and text. For this example, I will start with the Odd Page Header.

Once you are in your header section, you will also see a "Header and Footer Tools" tab which appeared near the top of your Microsoft Word screen. In this menu bar, click the "Page Number" button, and select "Top of Screen" from the first drop-down menu, and then pick which formatting your want for your header. Which one? Well, I choose one with the Chapter Heading Text built right in, and then change the formatting on it later. But if you want to just select the pager number and then add chapter heading text on your own later to the header section, that is fine too. Just play around with it until you get what you like. And because I am adding numbers and text to the Odd Page Header, I choose the Page Number and Header text that is aligned to the right.

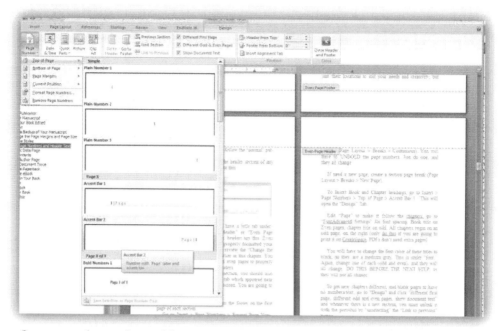

Once you have done this, you will see that page numbers and header text have been added throughout your manuscript to the odd-numbered pages. Now you will want to the repeat the process for the even-numbered pages, while making sure that you choose the opposite location for the header numbers and text. When done, it will look something like this:

Your heading may look a little bit different, but you can change the formatting and style of these headers to match however you want them to look. For my headings, I change the font color to black, remove the lower border, and make each header follow the "First Paragraph" Style. That way, my header section follows the styling in the rest of the book.

If you scroll through your book manuscript, you should see that nearly every odd-numbered page has the header text and page number on the top right, and nearly every even-numbered page has the header text on the top left. If you set up your manuscript properly, the first page of each section should be the only pages without any header page numbers or page headings. In other words, the first page of each chapter should show no page number or header text. If there are page numbers and header text on the first pages of each section, go back and review how to create new sections for each chapter, and also make sure that you have selected the "Different First Page" option for each section. To make sure you have set this up correctly, you can go through the various sections of your manuscript, and double-click in the header section. When you do, the "Header and Footer Tools" menu will open up, and you should see that the "Different First Page" option has been selected, as well as the option for "Different Odd & Even Pages."

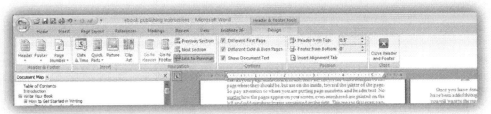

As long as we are on this image, note the highlighted button which says, "Link to Previous." That button becomes very important as we update the title and chapter headings throughout the book, which we turn to next.

To add the book title and chapter headings, start by going to the very first page of your manuscript, and scrolling through the document page by page inspecting the header on each page. If the page looks fine, scroll on to the next page. Keep scrolling until you find a page that has some header text which is not correct. Maybe the header text is missing, or maybe the header text is showing where it should not be, or maybe it is showing, but it says the wrong thing. Here is a guide which shows what should be on each page throughout the document:

Front Pages (All pages up to Preface or Introduction)	No page numbers and no header text of any kind.
First Page of Each Chapter	No page number or header text of any kind. A footer page number is allowed.
Even-Numbered Pages	A page number and header text showing the Book Title. These are usually left-justified.
Odd-Numbered Pages	A page number and header text showing the Chapter Title. These are usually right-justified.
Even-Numbered Blank Page Before New Chapter	No page numbers and no header text of any kind. This page should be completely blank.

Before you start changing the header text on certain pages, you need to understand how sections work in Word, and what the settings mean when you told each section to have a Different First Page and a Different Odd & Even pages. As a result of these settings, each individual section has three main parts: a first page, odd-numbered pages, and even-numbered pages.

Before you start changing the header text on certain pages, you need to understand how sections work in Word,

Furthermore, all of these section parts throughout the entire document are linked. So all first pages are linked together, all odd-numbered pages are linked together, and all even-numbered ages are linked together. This means that if you make a change to one of the First Pages anywhere in the book, that change will get mirrored in all First Pages throughout the book. This is fine if you want to make a change to the entire document, but it is not fine if you want different sections to have different elements. If you want different elements in different sections, all you have to do is unlink a particular part of a section, both from what precedes and from what follows.

If you make a change to one of the First Pages anywhere in the book, that change will get mirrored in all First Pages throughout the book.

When you start scrolling through your book, the first place where you might notice something amiss is on the second page of the Table of Contents. Since it is the second page of a section, and it is an even-numbered page, it has header text and a page number in the upper left corner.

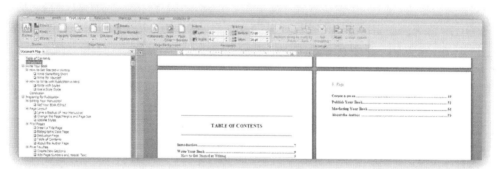

Since the Table of Contents is in the "Front Matter" area of the book, you don't want any page numbers or header text of any kind. But before you double-click in the header section and delete the header text and page number from this page, you first need to make sure that you will not also delete all the page numbers and header text from the rest of the manuscript. If you delete the page number and header text here, this will also delete the page numbers and header text on all even-numbered pages throughout the entire document because they are all linked. So you need to unlink them.

To unlink these sections, first go to the *second page* of the *next section* in your document, and double-click in the header section there. On my book, since my Table of Contents is in Section 7 and I want to delete the header text and page number from the second page in Section 7 (which is an even-numbered page), I first go to the second page of Section 8 (which is also an even-numbered page), and double-click in the header there. If Section 8 was only one page long, then I would go to the second page of Section 9 (which should be an even-numbered Page). Essentially, on your own book, you want to find the *next* occurrence of the same *type* of page.

When you find it, double-click in the header so that the Header and Footer Toolbar opens, and you will see this screen again:

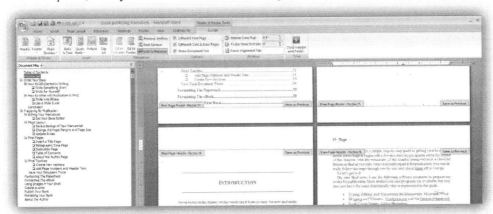

To unlink this page of the section from the one you are going to edit, simply click that "Unlink to Previous" button so that it is *not highlighted*. When you do this, the little blue tab which says "Same as Previous" will disappear. Note that in the screenshot below, the "Link to Previous" button is no longer highlighted, and the blue "Same as Previous" tab in the header of page 10 is no longer there.

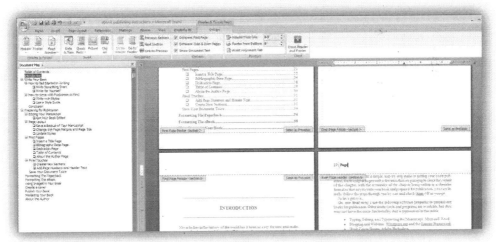

Now that you have unlinked the section that follows the one you want to edit, you need to unlink everything that came before it as well. To do this, you go back to the section you want to edit, which in this example is the second page of the Table of Contents, and double-click in the header section there, causing the Header and Footer Toolbar to open again, and then clicking the "Unlink to Previous" button again so that it is not highlighted.

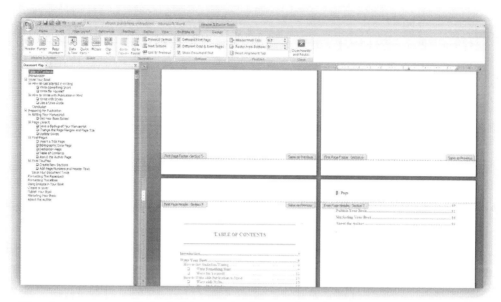

You have now unlinked this particular section header from everything that came before it and everything that follow it, which means you can edit it safely. When you delete that header text and page number, doing so does not delete all the header text and page numbers from every even-numbered page throughout the entire manuscript.

These are the steps you will follow throughout the rest of the manuscript. As you can tell, it is very easy to make a mistake in this process, so go slow, and after every change you make, double-check the preceding and following sections of your manuscript to make sure that everything is formatted properly.

It is very easy to make a mistake in this process, so go slow, and after every change you make, double-check the preceding and following sections of your manuscript to make sure that everything is formatted properly.

Let me show you how I follow these steps to add the book title to the even-numbered pages throughout the manuscript, and the chapter titles to the odd-numbered pages.

First, since the book title doesn't change, and it will always go on the even-numbered pages of every section throughout the document, I do not need to unlink these sections anywhere. I can just double-click in any even-numbered header, and enter the book title next to the page number.

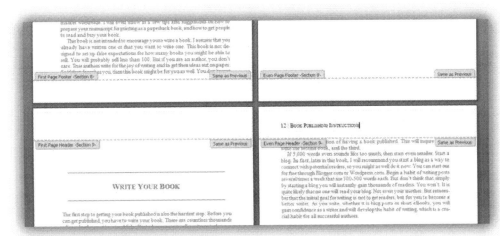

In the example above, I styled the book title so that it was written in SMALL CAPS. This won't translate well over into the eBook versions, but it looks good in the paperback edition. If you followed all the steps above properly, and you scroll through your manuscript, you should see that all of your even-numbered pages now have the book title in the upper left hand corner. That was simple!

So now you can add the chapter titles. Since you want the chapter titles to change with each new chapter, you need to make sure you unlink each new chapter from the preceding and following chapters, as you learned how to do earlier. Normally you would start with the Introduction to the book, but since the Introduction in this book is only two pages long, it only has a first page and an even-numbered page. It does not have an odd-numbered page. If your introduction is more than two pages, start there. Otherwise, go to the first chapter of the book and scroll down until you come to the first odd-numbered page which has the header text. Unlink it from everything that came before it, and then go to the first odd-numbered page of Chapter 2, and unlink it from the odd-numbered pages of Chapter 1. Finally, return to the first odd-numbered page of Chapter 1, and enter your chapter heading text for that chapter. Then repeat this process for the rest of the chapters in the book.

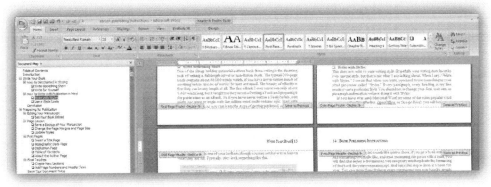

Note that this time on my book, rather than put it in SMALL CAPS, I entered the chapter title in *Italics*. My book now has the book title, the chapter titles, and page numbers on all the pages that require them.

Once all the chapter headings are added, you can a page number to the first page of each chapter. This is an optional step. Not all books have a page number of the first page of each chapter, but if they do, they are usually in the footer. And since all first pages of each section are linked, you only need to unlink all the Front Matter pages from the first page of the Introduction (or Preface). After that, all the first pages of each chapter can follow the same pattern, and there-fore, can remain linked.

To add this page number, go to the first page of the Introduction of your book and double-click in the footer area. This opens up the "Header and Footer" toolbar. Before clicking the "Page Number" button, make sure you click the "Link to Previous" button so it unlinks this first page from all the previous first pages in the book. Then, to add page numbers to all the linked first pages which follow, click on the "Page Number" button and select the page number that is centered.

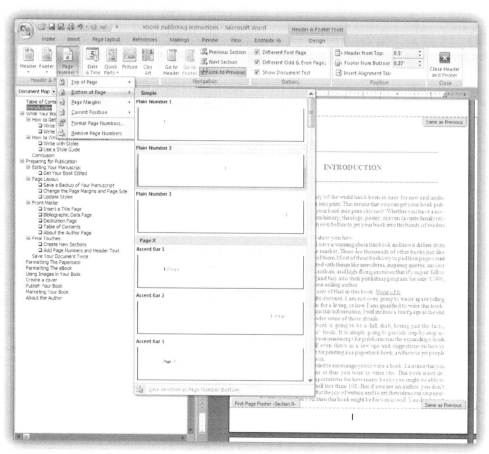

You may have to select the "Centered" Style from your Style settings, and do some additional formatting to make it look proper, but once it looks good, go and check to make sure that all the first pages of each subsequent section have the page number centered in the bottom as well. If you have any blank pages throughout your manuscript, you will probably need to delete the footer page number on those pages by unlinking them from what precedes and what follows, and then deleting the page number in the footer of those blank pages.

Once you have finished all the steps in this chapter, you are ready to format the manuscript for publication as a paperback book and various forms of eBook. However, since those processes can create many problems to your manuscript, there is one final step you should take in preparing your manuscript for publication.

❑ Save Your Document Three Times

In later chapters, you will create one set of files for publishing your manuscript as a paperback, and a second set of files for publishing your manuscript as an eBook. Since you have put so much work into creating the manuscript as it is now, and since formatting your manuscript for printing and for eBooks can mess up the formatting pretty quickly, it is wise to save a backup copy of your manuscript. In fact, while you are at it, make two additional copies of the manuscript, one for the paperback edition of the book, and one for the eBook editions.

For myself, I save the document first with its book title, then I save it again and add the word "paper" on the end, and then save it a third time with the word "ebook" on the end. This helps me know which file is which in the following steps. The files look like this in Windows Explorer:

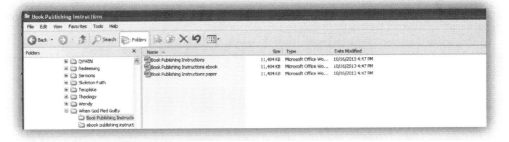

CREATE A COVER

Now that the interior pages of the book are finished and ready for publication, you need to create a cover. At this point, you will need to decide if your book is going to be published as a digital eBook only, or if you will also be printing paperback copies of the book. If you are only doing one or the other, you only need one cover file. But if you are publishing both, you will need to create two separate cover files. The reason is that while eBooks only need a front cover image, paperback books also require a spine and a back cover.

The process of creating a cover can be quite time-consuming and frustrating if you do not know what you are doing. So really, the first step in creating a cover is deciding whether you are going to create it yourself, or if you are going to hire someone else to create the cover for you. The minimum cost for having someone else create a cover for you is a couple hundred dollars, but the benefit is that you usually end up with a professional looking cover. The benefit to creating a cover on your own is that it is usually much cheaper, but the drawback is that the cover often looks cheap. As people often judge books by their covers, you need to decide what is best for you.

For my own publishing projects, I have always designed the covers myself. This is not because I think I am a good graphic design artist and can make good covers, but because I simply do not have the money to pay someone else to do the covers for me. I assume that most self-published authors are in the same boat, and so I am writing this chapter to reveal the steps I take in creating my own covers (You can see them here: Jeremy Myers on Amazon). If you want to skip this chapter and pay someone else to create your covers for you, that is fine. I recommend starting at Elance.com to see what is available.

The rest of this chapter will briefly explain a few tips for creating a cover, but I will include hardly any images or screenshots on how this is done. This is partly because explaining the actual process of creating a cover for your book is too complicated for this short guide. I will provide a few tips and suggestions to keep in mind as you go along, but you will have to figure out the actual graphic design part of the process on your own, or, as I suggested above, hire someone to do it for you.

❏ Find a Cover Image

The first step to creating a cover is to find a cover image. As with finding images to include in the interior of your book, you need to make sure that the image you use for you cover is not under Copyright (or you purchase the right to use it if it is) and that you will not have to pay royalties on the image every time it appears in print. To find such images, I recommend that you begin by using the same sites I recommended earlier in the book for locating book interior images.

One thing to look for while searching for cover images is that the image must be a high-quality, high-resolution image that will look good when printed. Most website images will provide the image dimensions in inches and pixels. At the absolute bare minimum, the image needs to be at least 1000 pixels on the shortest side, though 1500 pixels or more is preferable.

Also, while you are looking for a cover image, it is helpful to imagine and plan your cover layout. Depending on how you want your cover to look, maybe you don't even need an image. Or maybe you need two or three images. The best way to proceed is to look at the covers of several books on your shelves and how those covers were designed. Decide what you like or don't like about them, then start to brainstorm on your own about how you want your cover to look. I always get out a scratchpad and draw out several different types of covers with different layouts and designs.

I have also found it helpful to look at some recent cover designs online. I might go browse Amazon listings, or visit other websites that show book covers. For example, BookCoverArchive.com is a site which shows a lot of book covers. It doesn't have all book covers, but has well over 50,000 book covers to browse through. If you are looking for Christian book covers, I sometimes visit Lion's Gate Book Design and Hearts and Minds Books.

❏ Designing the eBook Cover

To design my eBook covers, I use Adobe Photoshop. You may be able to find free tools online, but they will probably not give you the design controls that you need. If you cannot afford Photoshop (the full version), you are probably better off paying a Graphic Design artist to make your cover for you.

One alternative is to use Amazon's Kindle Direct Publishing cover design process, but since I have never used it, I am not sure how well it works and cannot provide a recommendation or a guide for this process. Furthermore, since you want to make your books available not just through Amazon, but also on Barnes & Noble, and Apple iBooks, Amazon's cover design process may not be the best route.

Whichever way you choose to design your cover, the main thing is to make sure that you create a high-resolution cover which has the same dimensions as your page. You want you cover resolution to be about 300 dpi (dots per inch), and so multiply 300 by the width and height of your book which you set up under the Page Layout section of the previous chapter. Most of my books are 5.5 x

8.5 inches, and so I usually make my eBook cover dimensions to be 1650 x 2550 pixels. This current book is a little bit larger. The paperback version of this book is 7 x 10 inches, and so I created the cover image to be 2100 x 3000 pixels.

Once your cover has been created, you will want to save your file in a format that allows you to edit it later if necessary (.psd for Photoshop), and a file for using on your website or for using at the various places you send your eBook for distribution (.jpg is recommended). Sometimes you will need different sizes of these images for different purposes. For example, I have a sidebar widget on my personal blog which shows my book covers, and these covers are all 97x150 pixels. So I create a cover image of that size for my blog. Basically, now that you have your image, you can resize it or put it in advertisements for marketing purposes, or post the image on Facebook for feedback.

❏ **Designing the Paperback Cover**

Designing the cover for the paperback can get extremely tricky. As with creating the eBook cover, I strongly recommend you use a professional grade photo editing program such as Adobe Photoshop. If you are unable to do this, you are better off hiring someone else to design your cover for you. While you may be able to create an eBook cover with free or cheap photo editing software, the paperback cover requires greater attention to detail and precision than is usually available with most of those free programs. You not only need to design the front cover image, but also the back cover and the spine. The spine, of course, needs to be an exact width so that it properly encases all the pages of your book. It is not good to have a spine that is one inch wide if the actual thickness of your book is only half an inch. Furthermore, book printers need a border around your entire cover called a "bleed" so that when the book is trimmed, the cover still looks decent, even if the trim was off by an eighth of an inch.

Maybe the place to start is by defining the terms. The "Trim" size of the book is how tall and wide your book will be. It is essentially the same size as the "Page Layout" dimensions which were set up earlier in this guide. The "Spine" of the book is the part of the cover which wraps around the bound edge of the book, connecting the front cover to the back cover, and holding all the pages in place. The "Bleed" is the part of the cover which prints off the edge of the cover of the book, most of which will get trimmed off by the printer.

The first step in creating your paperback cover is to figure out the necessary dimensions. Since you already know the width and height of the pages, and the bleed width should be at least 0.125 inches, all you really need to do is calculate the width of the spine, and then add everything up to get the proper dimensions for the entire cover. But the problem is that different printers use different types and weights of paper, and the width can also be affected by whether or not your interior pages are printed in color or in black and white. To calculate the width of your spine, you need to contact your printer to get the proper measurements for the paper that they use.

For my own printing needs, I use either Amazon's CreateSpace or Ingram's Lightning Source to print and distribute books. I will explain why later. If you are going to use CreateSpace, you can calculate the spine width of your book on this page: CreateSpace spine and cover width. If you use Lightning Source, they have a nifty Lightning Source Spine Width Calculator which you can use. For example, CreateSpace says their page thickness is 0.002252 inches, so I calculate my total book thickness by multiplying 0.002252 by the total number of pages in my book.

Just by way of clarification, some people get confused about what is meant by "page count." Is this the number of sheets of paper in your book, or the actual number of "pages" that your book has? For example a 200 page book actually only has 100 sheets of paper since each sheet of paper has text on both sides. So when calculating the width of the spine, should you calculate it based on the number of sheets of paper in the book, or the actual page count? The answer is to use the actual page count, *not* the number of sheets of paper in your book. Since every piece of paper has two sides, the number of pages in your book should always be an even number.

Now that you have the spine width for your book, you are ready to calculate the entire cover size. Calculate the width first. The width of your paperback cover is as follows:

Bleed + Page Width + Spine + Page Width + Bleed

So if your book page width is 5.5 inches, and has 200 pages, your cover width calculation is as follows:

0.125 + 5.5 + (200 x 0.002252) + 5.5 + 0.125

This gives you a cover width of 11.7004 inches.

Calculating the height of the paperback cover is a bit easier. All you need is the height of the book plus the top and bottom bleed:

Bleed + Page Height + Bleed

If the page height is 8.5 inches, then your paperback cover calculation is as follows:

0.125 + 8.5 + 0.125

This gives a cover height of 8.75 inches. So the cover dimensions for the 5.5 x 8.5 paperback with 200 pages are 11.7004 inches wide by 8.75 inches high. These are the dimensions you will need to enter into Photoshop or give to your graphic design artist who is creating the cover for you.

Of course, even though these are the dimensions of the cover, it is critical to remember that you do not have this entire area to work with. Remember, about 0.125 inches are going to get trimmed off of every side of the cover, and sometimes, this trimming process can be off by about that much again. This means that you should not have required text or graphics that come within 0.125 inches of the trim size of your book. In other words, no required text or images should be within .25 inches of your outermost edge.

This is also true of any text you wish to put on the spine of your book. During the printing and trimming process, the spine area can be offset left or right by as much as 0.125 inches either way, though usually the spine drift is less than 0.0625 inches. You need to keep this in mind as you design the cover. If your front cover is black, and the spine is white, it is quite possible that the spine area will not get placed exactly where you want it in the printing and trimming process, and some of that black front cover will end up on the spine, or some of the white spine area might show up on the front cover. Therefore, it is best, if possible, to not include any vertical lines, hard edges, or color

It is best, if possible, to not include any vertical lines, hard edges, or color changes on the spine of your book.

changes on the spine of your book. It is quiet unlikely that the color change which you wanted on the fold line of the cover will appear exactly on the fold line.

Note that spine drift isn't necessarily an indication of a bad print job. If you carefully inspect the books in your library, you will see that book covers which have a hard line color change for the spine often have some small carry-over from the spine onto the front or back over. Most readers aren't going to care about this too much, and maybe you don't either, but it is something to think about as you prepare your cover for printing.

But it is not just the colors on the spine that require careful planning. If your spine text fills the entire spine area, it is possible that some of your spine text will end up on the front or back cover. This is a very noticeable mistake. But with a little planning, it can be avoided. The text on your spine needs to have at least 0.0625 inches of padding on either side of it so that some of the spine text does not end up on the front or back cover.

> *It is not just the colors on the spine that require careful planning. If your spine text fills the entire spine area, it is possible that some of your spine text will end up on the front or back cover. This is a very noticeable mistake. But with a little planning, it can be avoided.*

Think about what this means for short books. If the text on the spine requires 0.0625 inches of padding on either side (0.125 inches total), and due to a small page count, your spine was only 0.25 inches to begin with, this means your spine text can only be 0.125 inches in height! That is some tiny spine text. So my recommendation is that if your page count is less than 100 pages, don't even try to print it as a paperback; just be happy with publishing it as an eBook. If, however, you absolutely *must* print a book with less than 100 pages, don't put any text on the spine. Doing so will only mean that your spine text is too small to read.

It is also important to leave room for the barcode on the back cover of your book. You will need an area about 2.25 x 1.5 inches on the lower right-hand corner of the book's back cover for the barcode. Make sure that no important images or text are in this area, as they will be covered by the barcode.

Other than this, there are not too many tips and suggestions I can give for creating your paperback book cover. Note that if you want to print a hardback book with a dust jacket, this will require even further calculations and design work. CreateSpace does not offer this option, so if you want to create hardback copies of your book, this is when you will need to use Lightning Source. They have a detailed guide about how to <u>create hardback and dust jacket cover files for printing</u>.

Once your cover is created, you will want to save it in various formats, just as you did with the eBook cover file. Make sure you save a file which allows for future editing (.psd for Photoshop) and a file for using on your website or for using at the various places you send your eBook for distribution (.jpg is recommended). Whoever is printing your book will also require a PDF document for printing. CreateSpace and Lightning Source both require a PDF document of your cover, which has the fonts embedded within the document.

❏ **Create a 3D Cover Image for Marketing Material**

After your cover images are finished, it is also a good idea to create some marketing material for your book. Yes, even if you are not planning on paying for any marketing, you will probably at least want to put a picture up on your blog or on Facebook. And while you could just put a plain picture of the front cover, it is sometimes a good idea to show something a little nicer as well.

For example, you might want to create a few small banners which show the book cover, along the title, a brief description, and a location for where the book can be purchased.

One thing I really recommend is that you turn your book cover into a 3D cover image. No, not one of those images that are blurry until you put on the special 3D glasses, but one of those images which appear to be standing on end with the pages slightly open. These images are very eye-catching and will help draw people's attention to your book.

But how do you create one of these? By far the best way to do this is with a Photoshop plugin called <u>Cover Action Pro</u>. Of course, to use it, you have to own Photoshop, and so once again, this might not work for you. Let me offer a service to you though. If you have a book cover already made which you would like to have transformed into one of the Cover Action Pro templates, contact me through Redeeming Press with what you are looking to do, and for a small one-time fee, I can generate the 3D cover of your choice. Just go to <u>Cover Action Pro</u> and select the "Paperback book" style that you want, and then get in touch with me for further details.

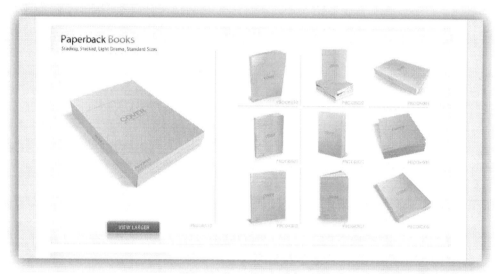

If you do own Photoshop, here are the steps I follow to turn my cover images from above into a 3D cover using Cover Action Pro (and after installing the Cover Action Pro Photoshop Actions).

First, I open Photoshop and go to Actions on my sidebar to select the action I want to perform. If they are not showing, you can get this window to appear by Clicking on "Window" from your toolbar, and selection "Actions" from the drop-down menu. My preferred actions are PBOOK002 (a stack of books) and PBOOK008 (a single book standing on its side).

In the Action window, I open the Action I am going to use and then select the "Create" option and click the "Play" icon at the bottom. The Photoshop Action does its thing, leaving a template on the screen. I fill in the pieces it asks for on the front of the book and on the spine. When I am done, I select "Render" on the Action window, and then click "Play" again. In just a few seconds, it creates a beautifully rendered 3D image of my book, which is perfect for putting on my blog, sending to Facebook, or for creating banner ads. I save it as a .psd file in my book folder which I am working on, flatten the image, and then save it as a .jpg for use on my sites. For example, I often create a 300 pixel wide image of this 3D book cover for the Bookstore on Redeeming Press.

Though creating books covers is a time-consuming aspect to preparing your book for publication, it is a vital aspect as well, for whether you like it or not, people will judge your book by its cover.

FORMAT THE PAPERBACK

Now that you have finished writing, editing, and typesetting your manuscript for publication, and you have a cover ready for printing, it is time to create the files needed to submit to Amazon, Apple iBooks, and anywhere else that you want to send the files for publication. This chapter will explain the steps necessary for creating a PDF file which will be used for the paperback editions of the book, and the next chapter will explain how to create the html files for all eBook editions, whether they are for the Kindle, Nook, or iPad.

You should have already saved your manuscript three times, one as a backup file which you can go back to in case something goes wrong, one to use as the paperback manuscript, and one to use for the eBook manuscript. This step should have been completed at the end of Chapter 2, and here is an example of what the three different files might look like in your document folder:

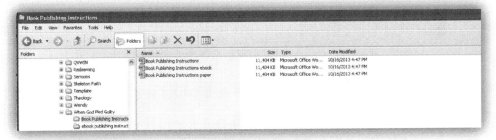

What you want to do is open the file that will be used for the paperback book. This is the document you are going to use to create the necessary files to send to Amazon CreateSpace or Ingram Lightning Source for printing.

❑ **Correct Pagination Issues**

If you followed all the steps in this book up to this point, only one thing needs to be checked before saving your file as a PDF for printing, and this usually only needs to be checked if you used images in your book. Subheadings and section headings can also cause these pagination issues, but images are the primary culprits. Images don't always fit perfectly on the page where you inserted one; they sometimes get pushed down to the top of the following page, leaving a big white space on the page where the image was originally inserted. Here, for example, is a screenshot from a page where I inserted an image, but because of its size, it got pushed down to the following page:

To fix this, I will have to add text to the page on which the image was supposed to go so that the paragraph text flows all the way to the bottom of the page. On an eBook, you don't have as much control over this, since the text and images flow according to the screen size and font size of the eReader being used. But in a paperback book, you can control all elements of the layout, and so if you used images in your book and have these big ugly blank spot on the page, here is how to remove them.

You can, if you want, simply add paragraph text until the text on the page fills all the way to the bottom. Usually, however, this is not feasible. The paragraphs of your chapter have a logical flow and you cannot just add a paragraph or two of filler text without messing things up. So the best option is to add a pull quote to your page. Pull quotes are snippets of text pulled from the paragraphs already on that page and quoted in a text box off on one side of the page. When book publishers include pull quotes in their books, it is not usually because they think the author made such a good point that it needed to be emphasized. The reason is because they were attempting to correct some sort of pagination issue in the chapter.

To add a pull quote to your page, go the "Insert" tab of Microsoft Word and click the "Text Box" button. A menu will appear which gives you various text box options for inserting. Pick one which fits your book theme best. For this book, I chose the Austin Pull Quote.

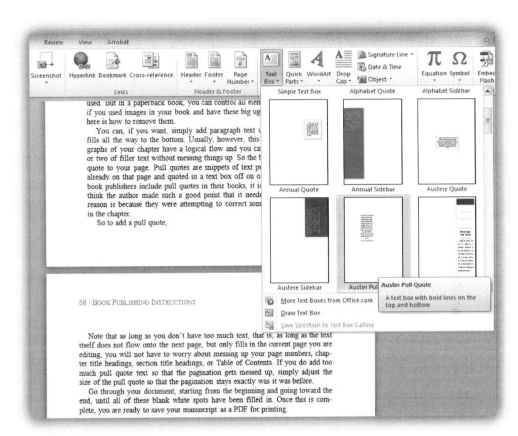

Once you inset the pull quote, select a quote from the page on which you are inserting it which is quote worthy, and type it into the pull quote text box. Make sure that you choose a quote which is long enough to cause the text on the page to fill the page, but not so long that it causes some of the text to spill over onto the next page. The reason is that you don't want to mess up your pagination.

As long as the text on the page does not flow onto the next page, but only fills in the current page you are editing, you will not have to worry about messing up your page numbers, chapter title headings, section title headings, or Table of Contents. If you do add too much pull quote text so that the pagination gets messed up, simply adjust the size of the pull quote so that the pagination stays exactly was it was before.

One other thing to note is the location of the pull quote on the page. If it is on an odd-numbered page, that page will get printed on the right-hand side of the book. Therefore, you probably want the pull quote on the right-hand side of the page, toward the outer edge of the book. Alternately, if the pull quote is on an even-numbered page, it should go on the left-hand side of the page so that when the book is printed, these quotes also will appear on the outer edge of the book.

Here is the page I showed above with the pull quote added to it so that the text fills the page but does not overflow on to the next page.

Go through your document, starting from the beginning and going toward the end until all of these blank white spots have been filled in. Once this is complete, you are ready to save your manuscript as a PDF for printing.

❑ Save the Manuscript as a PDF

If you are happy with the layout and look of your entire manuscript, all you really need to do is save the manuscript as a PDF. In Microsoft Word, this is done by Clicking the "Save As" button and then in the file format drop-down menu, selecting "PDF" from the available options. This should be available in Microsoft Word 2007 and following.

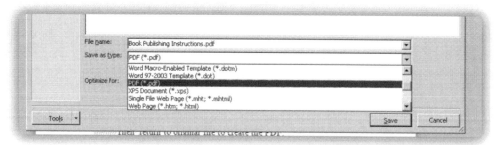

After selecting the PDF, and before clicking the "Save" button, remember to update Title and author options in "Save" screen (if they are available), and you will want to choose the "Standard" quality of PDF, which is used for publishing online and printing.

❑ **Embed Fonts in PDF (if necessary)**

If you used any creative fonts or typefaces in your manuscript, you should probably embed them into your PDF. Embedding fonts ensures that your PDF uses the same fonts as the original document, no matter who opens the PDF or what fonts are installed on their system. You can embed the fonts in Microsoft Word by going to the "File" menu item, going to very bottom and clicking "Options." A window will open up and in the "Save" section, click the "Embed Fonts in the file" option.

> *Embedding fonts ensures that your PDF uses the same fonts as the original document, no matter who opens the PDF or what fonts are installed on their system.*

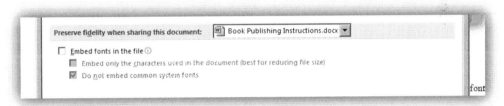

The one problem with this is that some premium fonts which you may have purchased will not properly embed this way. Font creators do not want their fonts to be passed around to people for free through embedded font files. And yet, printers need this font files for accurate printing. How do you know if a font file has not been properly embedded? When you upload your file to CreateSpace or Lightning Source, they will give you an error message that the PDF document contains a font which is not available at the printer. If this happens, you will need to embed the fonts through a different method, which requires the use of <u>Adobe Acrobat Professional</u>. This is different than the free Adobe Reader which is available on most computers. Adobe Acrobat Professional is the program which allows you to create and edit Adobe PDF documents. As with all the Adobe products, this program is quite expensive, and so if you do not own it and cannot afford it, it may be best to use fonts which do not require special embedding.

However, if you own Adobe Acrobat Professional, and you need to use its ability to embed fonts in a PDF, here is a brief guide on how to do this.

Open the PDF which you have just created with Adobe Acrobat Professional. From the main screen, choose the "Tools" option from the menu bar, and select "Content" and the "Edit Document Text" option.

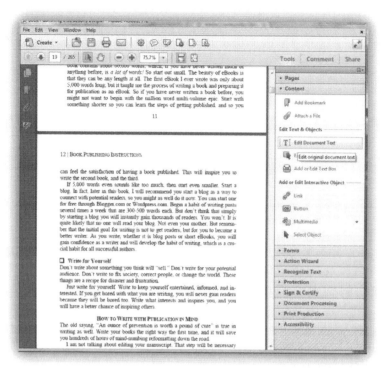

Click a section of text which contains the font you want to embed. Right-click this section with your mouse, and choose "Properties." In the "Touchup Properties" dialog box that opens, click the "Text" tab to display the font name and font properties as well as embedding and subset capabilities. This will open a list of fonts that are used throughout the document. Fonts that are used in the document are listed first, and other available fonts on your system are listed below the document fonts.

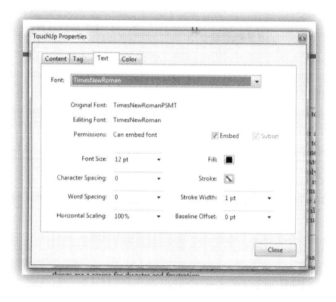

Choose a font from the Font menu that you want to embed. Once selected, it will show you what permissions are available for this font. Select which embedding option you want from those that are available. The options are usually these:

1. Can Embed Font—You can select both the Embed and Subset options. To embed the entire font rather than a subset, make sure that Subset is not selected.
2. Can Embed Font For Print And Preview Only—You can only subset-embed the font. You can embed the font for print and preview but not for editing.
3. Cannot Embed Font—Both the Embed and Subset options are unavailable.
4. No System Font Available—Both the Embed and Subset options are unavailable.

For book printing purposes, you should select the first option if it is available. If not, the second option will be fine, since it allows for printing and previewing, but not for editing. If the only available options are number 3 or 4, and CreateSpace is telling you that they need the embedded font, your only real option is to not use that font and select one which can be embedded into the PDF document.

When you are embedding the fonts using a similar method, click "Save" and the font should be embedded into your PDF. Other options can be done to your PDF at this point as well, such as converting your color profile to CMYK or to grayscale, flattening your images, or anything else that is required by Amazon CreateSpace, Ingram Lightning Source, or wherever else you print your book. Within Adobe Acrobat, you can use the Print Production Preflight options to find and correct any of these sorts of errors. You will know what is necessary because if something is missing from your file or if the printer needs something changed, they will let you know.

Some people want to know if they need crop marks, registration marks, or color bars on the PDF that they send in for printing. The answer is to check with your printer. Neither CreateSpace nor Lightning Source require these printing elements, and in fact, tell you to submit your PDF *without* such items. If you don't know what crop marks, registration marks, or color bars are, then you don't need them.

Once all the changes are done, you are now ready to upload your PDF to CreateSpace, Lightning Source, or wherever you are having your manuscript printed.

❑ Add Cover Image to PDF for Website Distribution

Some authors like to distribute the PDF manuscript through their website. While you definitely can use the PDF as it is right now, it is a good idea to add the eBook cover image to the PDF which you will be distributing on your website so that when people open the PDF, the first thing they see is a picture of the beautiful cover which you have designed.

Of course, you *do not* want this image as the first page of the PDF which you send to the printer. They will have a different method of uploading your cover files, and they want these files separate from the interior pages of the PDF. So if you decide to distribute the PDF through your website, you will need to create a second PDF document for that purpose.

> *There are two ways of adding your cover image to your PDF document.*

There are two ways of adding your cover image to your PDF document. The first (and best way), is to simply use the PDF which you have already created, and insert the eBook cover image as the "First Page" of the PDF. However, this requires the use of Adobe Acrobat Professional, and so if you do not have that program, you will need to use the second method below.

If you do have Adobe Acrobat Professional, use it to open the PDF you created in the previous step, and then from the Tools section, open the "Pages" options, and in the "Insert Pages" section, select "Insert from File."

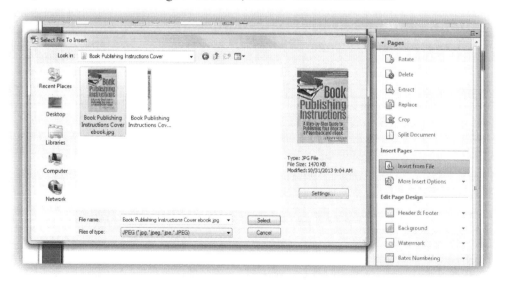

A window will open up which allows you to find the images or pages you want to insert. Navigate to where you saved the eBook cover image in .jpg format and select it. From the available options, choose to insert it "Before" the "First Page." Click OK, and you're done.

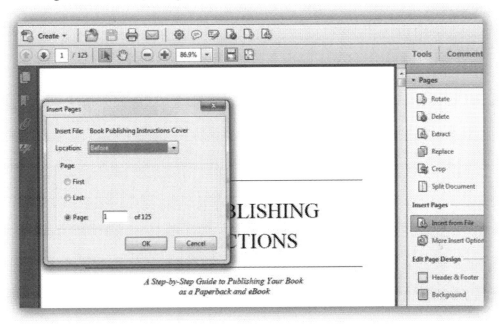

You will now want to save this second PDF with a slightly different file name so that you know which one is for uploading to your printer, and which one can be distributed through your blog or website.

The second way to insert the cover image on the first page is if you do not have Adobe Acrobat Professional, you can still insert your cover image into your PDF. But to do this, you will go back and use the original Microsoft Word document. Go to the very first page of the document, and insert a blank page.

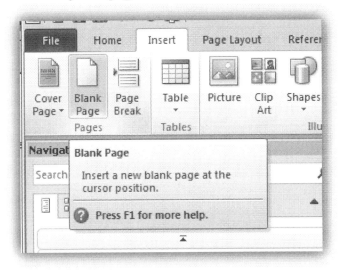

Then you can insert a picture onto this blank page, using the same methods as described in chapter 2 about inserting images into your document. Find the eBook cover .jpg file, and insert it onto your blank page. Then save the file as a PDF as described in this chapter, making sure to give it a different name than the PDF document you will be sending to your printer.

You now have your PDF documents for distributing on your website and for sending to your printer. But before you learn how to upload these files for publication, you need to learn how to format the manuscript and prepare the book files for publication as an eBook.

FORMAT THE EBOOK

Now that you have created the PDF for the paperback edition of the book, it is time to create the files needed for the Kindle, Nook, and iPad. The Kindle uses a file format called Mobi Pocket (.mobi), and the Nook and iPad use a file format called ePub (.epub). Concerned yet? Don't be. I will guide you through the process. Both types of files can be created from an HTML file (.html), and Microsoft Word can easily create one of these.

But before you begin, a recommendation is in order. While the process of turning your manuscript into an HTML file is rather simple, the process of editing your HTML file to turn it into an ePub file can get rather involved and complex. It can take hours of time, and be quite frustrating, *especially* if you know little about HTML. So here is my recommendation: Before you go through the hassle of creating and editing your HTML file, skip everything in this chapter about creating HTML files. Yes, skip it all. There are a few steps to take regarding your Word document, but if you want to test your luck with your Word document only, then these are the only steps you need to take. You can skip the rest about the HTML files. Remember that these steps are here, of course, in case you want to come back to it later, but it is possible that you may not need any of the information in this chapter beyond the few minor adjustments that need to be done to the Word document itself.

Here is why: Most eBook publishing platforms today will accept Microsoft Word documents. You can submit your Word document to Amazon, Barnes & Noble, and Smashwords. There is even one method of submitting a Word document to Apple. Smashwords will list your book on Barnes & Noble and Apple iBooks, so really, between Amazon and Smashwords, you have most of your publishing bases covered.

If you followed the formatting guide pretty carefully above, your Word document has a good chance of being the only file you need to publish on these three platforms. Both Google and Apple require the ePub file format, which is created from the HTML file. I show you how to create the HTML file in the rest of this chapter, but I recommend that before you go through the hassle of trying to create the ePub file without any errors, you first upload your Word document manuscript to Amazon and Smashwords to see how the book looks. They both allow you to "preview" the book before it is published, and so if you like the way your eBook looks and handles simply from uploading the Word document, then you don't have to worry about the content of this entire chapter! Advance to Go; Collect $200.

Whether you decide to create the HTML file or not, there are the few minor changes necessary which must be done to the Word document.

❑ Prepare the Word Document for Uploading

Before a Word document that can be uploaded to Amazon, Smashwords, and possibly Apple iBooks, you must remove certain elements from the document which can cause problems with those publishing platforms. This formatting also needs to be removed if you are going to create an HTML file.

To begin with, make sure you open the correct manuscript. At the end of Chapter 2 you created three files, one as a backup file which you can go back to in case something goes wrong, one to use as the paperback manuscript, and one to use for the eBook manuscript:

In the previous chapter you used the file created for the paperback edition and turned it into a PDF document. In this chapter, you will make some changes to the eBook file so that it uploads properly to the places that accept it, and can also be used to create the HTML file if you choose to go that route. So open the correct file in Microsoft Word.

Once it is open, you first need to make some minor adjustments to the Table of Contents. Currently, the Table of Contents has page numbers. But eReaders like the Kindle and iPad don't have page numbers. They format the page to the size of the screen, and flow the text through as many screens as needed to fit all the content. So you need to remove the page numbers from the Table of Contents.

Now if you were just to save your document as an HTML document, it would *appear* that Word removed the page numbers from the Table of Contents. But it doesn't. It only hides them. Word *does* remove the page numbers on each individual page, but it leaves the page numbers in the Table of Contents. They will not appear on the screen, but if you inspect the HTML code, they get left in. These hidden page numbers then cause problems and create errors later on in the process of publishing an eBook. So you want to remove the page numbers in the Table of Contents completely.

To do this, scroll down in your open Word document to your Table of Contents. Then, go to the "References" tab in your Word document, and click the "Table of Contents" button. A drop-down menu will appear, and near the bottom, click the "Insert Table of Contents" button. You already have a Table of Contents, but this will replace it with a new one. In the new Table of Contents, you do not want any page numbers, so in the window that appears, uncheck the box which says "Show page numbers." Click "OK" and your Table of Contents will update, this time without any page numbers. It will ask you if you want to replace the current Table of Contents, which, of course, you do.

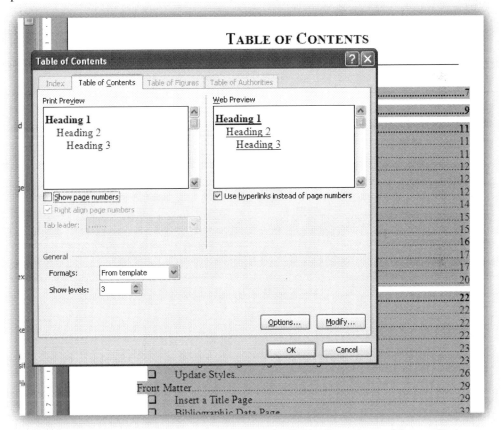

Your Table of Contents will now appear as it did before, but without all the page numbers, and without the dotted tab leaders (if use used them).

The second thing that needs to be done to your Word document is to go through and remove all the blank pages that were included at the end of chapters. If you remember, we added blank pages at the end of chapters whenever the chapter ended on a right-hand page. The reason is because most books have the first page of a new chapter begin on a right-hand page, and to make this happen, a blank page on the left-hand side of the book was needed. But eBooks do not have left and right-hand pages. They only have a screen. When people read books on a screen, it is not desirable to have a blank screen. So you need to go through and remove all those extra blank pages. To do this, simply find a blank page you want to delete, and then put your cursor at the end of the very last line of the preceding page, and press the "Delete" button on my keyboard. I cannot really show screen shots on how to do this, but here is how your pages should look from one chapter to another:

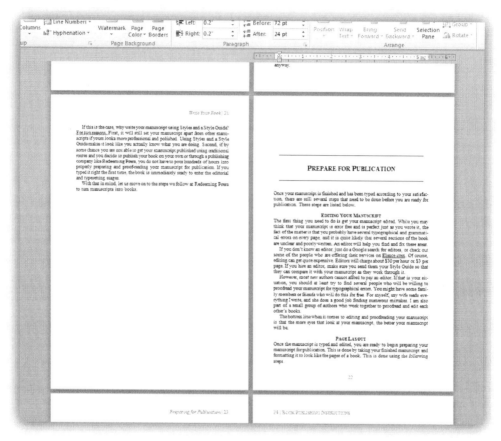

Go through your entire document and get rid of all extra blank pages just as shown above. Once this is done, you have finished making the necessary edits to your Word document. This Word document can now be uploaded as it is to Amazon, Smashwords, and even in one of the methods for Apple iBooks.

If, however, you find that you don't like the way your eBook looks when you upload the Word document to those platforms, you will probably have to transform your Word document into an HTML file, which can then be uploaded to Amazon, or changed into an ePub file which can be uploaded to Barnes & Noble, Google Books, and Apple iBooks. I encourage you to try to the Word document first, and if it looks strange, then come back and follow the rest of the instructions in this chapter.

❑ Save Your Manuscript as HTML

To create the HTML file, you still need to have completed the two minor edits to the Word document which were described in the previous section. Once those two changes are complete, you can save your Word document as an HTML document. To do this, go to the "File" tab in Microsoft Word, click "Save As" and then in the window that opens up, select "Web page, Filtered" from the drop-down menu. Click "OK" and you're done.

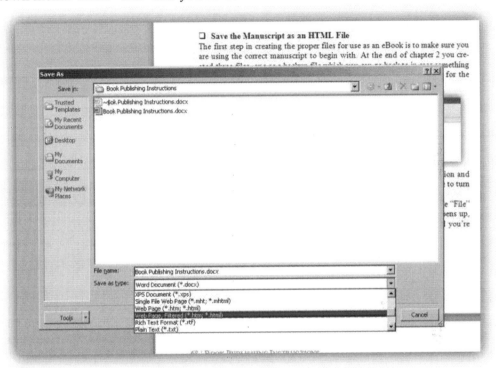

Make sure you select the Web Page, Filtered option, and not the "Single File Web Page" or the regular "Web Page" option. You could probably use these files, but Microsoft inserts a bunch of unnecessary code into the file with these other options, and you want your HTML file to be stripped down as much as possible. The "Web Page, Filtered" option will provide exactly what you need.

If you check your file location folder now, you should see an .html (or .htm) file along with the Microsoft Word documents. Also, if your manuscript has embedded images, saving your document as

If your manuscript has embedded images, saving your document as a Filtered Web Page will not only create the HTML file, but will also create a folder which contains all the embedded images.

a Filtered Web Page will not only create the HTML file, but will also create a folder which contains all the embedded images. This will be important later when you prepare to upload the document to Amazon.

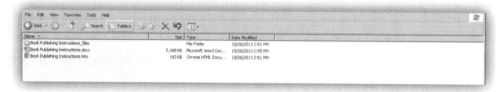

If you want to open up this newly created HTML file, just double click on it, and it will open with whatever web browser you have selected as your default browser. When I double click on the HTML file, it shows me this:

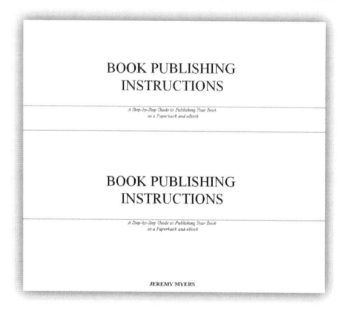

If you scroll through this file, you should see all your images in there, along with the text of your book, the chapter divisions, and everything else you have written and prepared. It should look and act somewhat like a very basic web site.

❏ Edit the HTML File

After creating the HTML file, you will need to edit it. But Microsoft Word is not the best tool for this job. While you can open and edit the HTML file with Microsoft Word, the program does not have a good way of editing the actual HTML code of the file, which is what you need to do. If you have never looked at much HTML, this could sound daunting, but hopefully the steps suggested below will guide you through what you need to know for editing your HTML document.

Before you begin editing the HTML file however, rename the file so that it does not have any spaces. You probably know that website addresses do not allow spaces in the URLs. This applies to your HTML file as well. So in place of the space in your file name, put dashes (-) or underlines (_). I renamed the HTML file for this book by adding (_) to the spaces so that it was named Book_Publishing_Instructions.

After you have renamed it, you are now ready to edit it.

Of course, before you edit your HTML file, you will need a decent HTML editing program. My preferred HTML editing program is Notepad++, which also happens to be free, which makes it even better. You can <u>download Notepad++ here</u>. Just download it using the button on the left, and then install it onto your computer as you would any other program.

Before you edit your HTML file, you will need a decent HTML editing program. My preferred HTML editing program is Notepad++, which also happens to be free, which makes it even better.

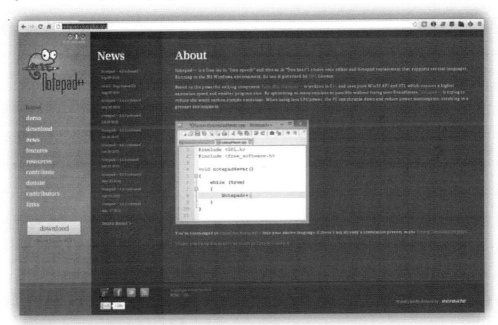

Once you have installed Notepad++, start the program and open the newly created HTML file which you made in the previous step. Unless you are somewhat familiar with HTML markup, the file will initially look like a bunch of gibberish. But if you take a few minutes to look through it, you will begin to see some common patterns to the HTML code which help you understand what is going on.

I am not able to explain all the elements of the HTML document which you are looking at, but simply notice that pretty much every part of the document is surrounded by bits of HTML code which tell the web browser (or in our case, the program which will be creating our eBooks) what to do with that part of the document. Relatively little of this has to be edited, but there are a few small sections that need some tweaks.

First, you should check the Title area of your document, which is all the way at the very top of the file. The Title area should be four or five lines down from the top, and should be surrounded by Title tags which look like this:

You can see that in the screenshot above, I changed the text inside the title tags to say "Title of Your New Book Should Go Here: Add Subtitle Also If You Want." You should type your own title into that area, and include the subtitle of your book in there as well if you have one. Make sure you leave intact the HTML title tags on either side of the book title.

After you are done with the title, you need to go through your document and remove all the extra section breaks that were added by Microsoft Word. Most of these should already be gone. They are created when you have blank pages in your document for extra pages in between chapters. Since you removed all these blank pages earlier in this chapter, there should be no more extra page breaks in your HTML document. But it doesn't hurt to check. While you are removing any extra page breaks that might remain, you also want to look for extra line breaks and remove them as well. You never want to have more than four line breaks in a row either, and so you will look for extra line breaks and remove those as well.

What you are looking for in the HTML code are Word sections that have no content. Here are some I found in my document:

```
586
587    <p class=CenteredNormal><i>Thanks for reading everything I write-no matter how
588    boring,</i></p>
589
590    <p class=CenteredNormal><i>and through it all, remaining my number one fan.</i></p>
591
592    <p class=MsoNormal> </p>
593
594    <p class=MsoNormal> </p>
595
596    </div>
597
598    <span style='font-size:12.0pt;font-family:"Times New Roman","serif"'><br
599    clear=all style='page-break-before:always'>
600    </span>
601
602    <div class=WordSection6></div>
603
604    <span style='font-size:12.0pt;font-family:"Times New Roman","serif"'><br
605    clear=all style='page-break-before:always'>
606    </span>
607
608    <div class=WordSection7>
609
610    <div style='border-top:solid windowtext 1.0pt;border-left:none;border-bottom:
611    solid windowtext 1.0pt;border-right:none;padding:20.0pt 0in 20.0pt 0in;
612    margin-left:.2in;margin-right:.2in'>
613
614    <h1 style='margin-top:1.0in;margin-right:0in;margin-bottom:24.0pt;margin-left:
615    0in'><span style='font-variant:normal !important;text-transform:uppercase'>Table
       of Contents</span></h1>
```

As you can see in the screenshot above, there is a span section with a style element of "page-break-before:always" in it. This tells the Kindle, iPad, and Nook to start a new page. This is good for new chapters and new sections of the book, but if you have two in a row, it is bad. As you can see above, I do have two in a row in my HTML. It looks like this:

```
<span style='font-size:12.0pt;font-family:"Times New
Roman","serif"'><br clear=all style ='page-break-
before:always'>
</span>
```

```
<div class=WordSection6></div>

<span style='font-size:12.0pt;font-family:"Times New
Roman","serif"'><br clear=all style='page-break-
before:always'>
</span>

<div class=WordSection7>
```

The two page break spans are separated by the WordSection6 div element. Also, the ePub file format does not like span elements. So you need to remove those as well, but keep the page break and one of the WordSection div elements. Once you do this, you are left with this:

```
<br clear=all style='page-break-before:always'>

<div class=WordSection7>
```

Doing so will remove the extra blank page on whatever eReader is being used. You need to go through your entire HTML document and search for double page breaks so you can remove one of them. Rather than scrolling through the entire document, it might be best to use the Notepad++ search feature and search for "WordSection" as the page breaks will always accompany the new section breaks.

After you have removed the extra page breaks and span elements, you will also want to remove any extra line breaks throughout your document.

After you have removed the extra page breaks and span elements, you will also want to remove any extra line breaks throughout your document. Sometimes when you type in Word, you hit the "Enter" button on your keyboard multiple times to properly space things. While this ends up looking okay in your paperback edition of the book, it can cause problems in the eBook editions. So remove any extra lines breaks where there is more than four line breaks in a row. A line break in HTML looks like this:

```
<p class=MsoNormal> </p>
```

I found one such section in my book where I had seven of these line breaks in a row. It was on my Dedication page:

```
563  <span style='font-size:12.0pt;font-family:"Times New Roman","serif"'><br
564  clear=all style='page-break-before:always'>
565  </span>
566
567  <div class=WordSection5>
568
569  <p class=MsoNormal> </p>
570
571  <p class=MsoNormal> </p>
572
573  <p class=MsoNormal> </p>
574
575  <p class=MsoNormal> </p>
576
577  <p class=MsoNormal> </p>
578
579  <p class=MsoNormal> </p>
580
581  <p class=MsoNormal> </p>
582
583  <p class=CenteredNormal><i>For my wife, Wendy.</i></p>
584
585  <p class=CenteredNormal><i> </i></p>
586
587  <p class=CenteredNormal><i>Thanks for reading everything I write—no matter how
```

To correct this, all I had to do was remove three or four of these line breaks. Note that there were only two breaks below the dedication to my wife, so to keep things even, I actually deleted five breaks from the top so that there were two above and two below. In the end, it looked like this:

```
<span style='font-size:12.0pt;font-family:"Times New
Roman","serif"'><br clear=all style='page-break-
before:always'>
</span>

<div class=WordSection5>

<p class=MsoNormal> </p>

<p class=MsoNormal> </p>

<p class=CenteredNormal><i>For my wife, Wendy.</i>
</p>

<p class=CenteredNormal><i> </i></p>

<p class=CenteredNormal><i>Thanks for reading every-
thing I write—no matter how
boring,</i></p>
```

```
<p class=CenteredNormal><i>and through it all, re-
maining my number one fan.</i></p>

<p class=MsoNormal> </p>

<p class=MsoNormal> </p>

</div>
```

As with the page breaks, you will want to go through your entire HTML document and search for places where you might have more than four line breaks, and remove any extra breaks. Again, use the search feature of Notepad++ to help accomplish this.

Next, you edit you need to do is only necessary if you used footnotes or endnotes in your document. Microsoft Word converts the footnote numbers into "Superscript" text, so that the little numbers rise above the rest of the text in the line, just as it does in your document. The problem with this is that it usually causes problems when you view the HTML file as a web page. So the easiest thing to do is simply to remove the superscript class from all the footnote and endnote numbers. Thankfully, you don't have to do this one by one. Just use the "Search" function in Notepad++ to find the lines that look like this:

```
span.MsoFootnoteReference
     {vertical-align:super;}

span.MsoEndnoteReference
     {vertical-align:super;}
```

You might have both of these sets of lines, or maybe just one. Either way, what you want to do is remove the "vertical-align:super;" part of the code, so that these sections look this way:

```
span.MsoFootnoteReference
     {}

span.MsoEndnoteReference
     {}
```

In this way, the footnote and endnote references will still be present within the file, and they will still link to the proper footnote location, but the numbers will be raised into superscript location, which caused strange things to happen to the document appearance. There are, of course, more advanced ways of handling these numbers, but this method is by far the easiest.

Also, related to footnotes, if you open up your manuscript HTML file with a web browser, you will probably notice that it dumped all your footnotes into the very end of the document. No matter what settings you used in your manuscript, converting the manuscript to an HTML file causes the footnotes to go to the end of the file, so that they appear as endnotes.

HTML documents cannot have footnotes at the bottom of a page, because different people will be using different screen sizes to view your document, and so there is no way of predicting how big their screen size will be, or where to put the footnote on the page. So your only options are to put your footnotes at the end of each chapter, or put all of them at the end of the book. Microsoft Word dumps them at the end of the document, but you can move them if you want. If you choose to move them, you will need to have some basic HTML editing knowledge.

Essentially, you need to find the section where all the footnotes have been placed, and copy and paste them one by one into the *end of the chapter* in which they are referenced. Then, you will also need to change the footnote numbers in the text and in the endnote reference so that they restart at "1" with each chapter, just as they do in a normal book. Of course, you do *not* want to change the HTML href bookmarks or names, because these must be unique to each footnote and each endnote reference throughout the entire manuscript.

Here is basically what I show at the end of my chapters when I move the footnote from the end of the book to the end of the chapter in which they appear:

```html
<p class=MsoNormal> </p>
<hr align=left size=1 width="33%">
<div id=edn15>
<p class=MsoEndnoteText><a href="#_ednref15"
name="_edn15" title="">
<span class=MsoEndnoteReference>
<span class=MsoEndnoteReference>
<span style='font-size:10.0pt;font-family:"Times New
Roman" ,"serif"'>[1]</span></span></span></a>
BOOK AUTHOR, <a href="BOOK URL GOES HERE"><i>BOOK TI-
TLE HERE</i></a>, (CITY, PUBLISHER: YEAR), PAGE
#.</p>
</div>
<p class=MsoNormal> </p>
</div><span style='font-size:12.0pt;font-
family:"Times New Roman","serif"'>
<br clear=all style='page-break-
before:always'></span>
<div class=WordSection7>
```

The following edits to the HTML document will help you in the conversion process to the ePub file format which is needed for Apple iBooks and a few other places. I will explain more about the ePub file format in a later chapter, but you can save yourself a lot of headaches and grief later by making a few minor adjustments to your HTML file now.

First, go the body tag of your HTML document, and if there are any "link" or "vlink" attributes here, remove them.

```
<body lang=EN-US link=black vlink=purple>
```

becomes

```
<body lang=EN-US>
```

Second, find and delete all the attributes which say "clear=all." What looks like this:

```
<br clear=all style='page-break-before:always'>
```

should become this:

```
<br style='page-break-before:always'>
```

To find and delete these quickly, I used the search and replace feature of Notepad++, make sure that I added a space after what I was search for, and put nothing in the replace window. That way, I didn't end up with extra spaces.

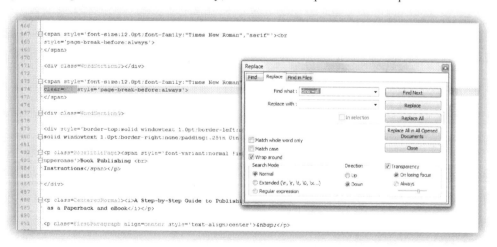

Third, the ePub files require that images do not have the border attribute. So I am going to use the search and replace function again to remove the border on all images. To do this, I search for this string:

```
<img border=0
```

and replace it with this:

```
<img
```

Fourth, the images are required to have alt tags. Since the images inserted by Word have id tags which are not needed, I am simply going to convert all the id tags into alt tags. To do this, I use the search and replace function again to search for this string:

```
id="Picture
```

and replace it with this string:

```
alt="eBook Publishing Picture
```

Note that in the example above, I also changed the text of the alt tag. Why? Alt tags describe what the picture is about, and since "Picture" is not very descriptive, I put added some keywords to the alt tags so that they are better describe the image that is being shown.

While you are replacing the id tags in your images with alt tags, you should also check to make sure that all images have alt tags. If there are images without alt tags, the ePub validator will issue an error.

Fifth, the ePub file format does not like a Table of Contents and interior hyperlinks which are identified with the "name" attribute. Instead, the ePub file format requires that the linked content be identified with the "id" attribute. So, using the search and replace function in Notepad++, I search for this string:

> *Alt tags describe what the picture is about, and since "Picture" is not very descriptive, I put added some keywords to the alt tags so that they are better describe the image that is being shown.*

```
name="
```

and replace it with this:

```
id="
```

Sixth, although you have just removed the "name" attributes, there is one you might want to put into your document. It is for the Kindle book, so if the ePub validator has a problem with it, just return and take it back out. The Kindle .mobi file likes to know where your Table of Contents is, and it does this by finding a "TOC" name tag in your document. To add it, insert the following line of code right before the Table of Contents:

```
<a name="TOC">
```

When this is done, the code right before your Table of Contents will look something like this:

```
<a name="TOC">
<h1 style='margin-top:24.0pt;margin-right:0in;margin-
bottom:24.0pt;margin-left: 0in'><a
id="_Toc374529902"><span style='font-variant:normal
!important; text-transform: uppercase'>Table of Con-
tents</span></a></h1>
```

Note that while this will enable the Table of Contents button to your Kindle eBook, it will not enable the Kindle Guide items. For that, you need a full Kindle OPF XML file, which can be created with the free Calibre program. This program will be examined later.

The edits to your HTML document are now complete. Hopefully, with the edits you have made, your eBook will not generate errors when you upload it to the sites that require it, or when you convert it to ePub and Mobi files.

❏ Compress Your Files

The last and final step of preparing your HTML document for submission to the websites for publication is to compress it into what is called a Zip file. Truthfully, this step is only required if your document had embedded images, videos, or other files. How can you know if you need to compress your manuscript into a Zip file? You can know by checking the location of your HTML file.

If you use Windows Explorer to examine the folder in which your HTML file is located, if you see another folder in that location which is the name of your book manuscript followed by "_files" then you know that you need to Zip up your HTML document and that folder with your files in it for submission to the eBook publishing websites. Since this document has images, you can see how Microsoft Word created a folder called "Book Publishing Instructions_files" in the folder with contains my "Book Publishing Instructions.htm" file. Those are the two files I need to Zip together and compress.

Again, if you don't see a folder that has "_files" on the end, then you do not need to do this step. You can simply submit your HTML file as it is, since it contains all the information that the eBook publishing sites will need.

If you do have the "_files" folder, then here is how to Zip up your document and that folder for submission. First, you need to select both the HTML document and the "_files" folder. You can do this by pressing and holding the Control (Ctrl) button, and then selecting both files with your mouse. Once both are selected, click your right mouse button, and a drop-down menu will appear. You want to go down and click the "Send To…" option, and from the new drop-down menu, select "Compressed (Zipped) Folder."

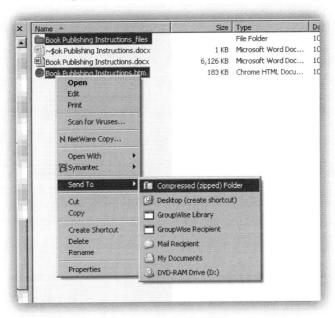

When you have done this, it will create the Zipped folder which contains your main HTML manuscript, and all the necessary files that go with it. It will look something like this:

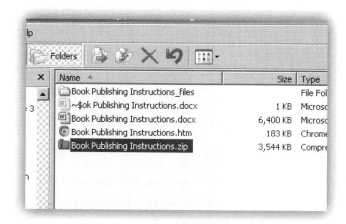

You are now done with formatting and creating the necessary files for your eBook. The only steps left are to upload them to the various websites which will be distributing your books, and then let people know you have published a book.

PUBLISH YOUR PAPERBACK

The step you have been working toward is now here. It is time to publish your book! In this chapter, you will publish your book as a paperback through Amazon CreateSpace and Ingram Lightning Source. The next chapter will provide instructions on publishing your book as an eBook on Amazon, Barnes & Noble, Google Books, Apple iBooks, and Smashwords. You do not need to publish your book on all of these platforms, but can pick and choose the ones that best fit your needs. The pros and cons of each will be explained as I go through each one.

❑ **Create a Book Information Document**
The first step, however, is to create a short Word document which contains the information and details about your book for the various publishing sites. While this document isn't absolutely necessary, putting all the information together at the beginning of the process will save you from having to track down the same information multiples times.

For my Book Information Document, I include the following details:

- Book title
- Book subtitle
- ISBN numbers for the various book editions
- Keywords for the book
- Categories for the book
- A brief description of the book (400 words or less)
- Author Biography

The Book title and subtitle are self-explanatory. You should already have the ISBN numbers from the earlier step of creating the Bibliographic Data Page in preparing your book for publication. The keywords are words and phrases which you think people might use to search for your book. There are a couple of ways to find the correct keywords and categories for your book. One way is to pretend you are searching for your book on Google or Amazon, and think about which words and phrases you would use to find your book. These words and phrases are the keywords you should use. You probably want about 5-10 of these keywords and key phrases.

The Categories for the book can be obtained from numerous sources, and each publishing site is going to be a bit different in how they categorize their books, but one way to get started is simply to search Amazon for books similar to yours, and then look at the category listings for those books. Find three or four of these books, and then scroll down to find the "Product Details" for the book. Most books on Amazon will show book categories for the book. Write down any that are applicable for your book. Here is the product listing for *How to Blog a Book*:

As you can see in the image above, there is a list of the book Best Sellers Rank with keywords and main categories for the book. These provides some good keywords for your your Book Information Document.

One extremely helpful site for book categories is the BISAC website. These are the standard codes and book categories used by the Book Industry Study Group. You can browse through the major list of subject here. Each section has numerous nested subsections, so just find one or two which most closely match your book subject. You may want to write down both the BISAC subject path, and the BISAC heading code. As will be seen later in this chapter, the Ingram Lightning Source publishing process has a beautiful search feature which allows you to easily find the best and most appropriate BISAC categories for your book. If you are having trouble figuring out which categories your book fits in, I highly recommend skipping ahead to the section in this chapter on publishing at Lightning Source so that you can use this search feature to find the best BISAC categories for your book.

Finally, type a brief book description for your book and a personal author biography. Try to keep both of these under 400 words, and the keywords you listed for your book should be included somewhere in the book description, and you might want to include your website details in your author biography. Make sure that you do not include the names of other books or other authors in your book description or keywords. Amazon frowns on this practice, and may delist your book if you do this. For example, if you are writing a legal mystery thriller, don't use the words "John Grisham" or any of his book titles in your keywords or book description.

Here is what my Book Information Document looks like for this book:

Book Publishing Instructions
A Step-by-Step Guide to Publishing Your Book as a Paperback and eBook

ISBN: 978-1-939992-16-1 (Paperback)
ISBN: 978-1-939992-17-8 (Mobi)
ISBN: 978-1-939992-18-5 (ePub)

Keywords:
book publishing, publish my book, publish ebooks, publishing guide, get published, write a book, become an author, Jeremy Myers,

Categories:
Writing, Research & Publishing Guides
Publishing & Books
Authorship
Books
eBooks
BISAC: Language Arts and Disciplines / Publishing - LAN027000

Book Description:
Get your book published this year! Use this step-by-step guide of book publishing instructions to turn your unpublished manuscript into a paperback book or an eBook for the Kindle, Nook, or iPad. Detailed descriptions of what to do are accompanied by screenshots for each step. Additional tools, tips, and websites are also provided which will help get your book published.

About the Author
Jeremy Myers is a popular author and blogger, and works as a publisher at Redeeming Press, a publishing company devoted to helping new and aspiring authors get their books into print. Jeremy can be contacted at RedeemingPress.com, or through his primary blog at TillHeComes.org.

Once your Book Information Document is ready, you can begin publishing your book at various locations. You will begin with guides for publishing your paperback book at Amazon CreateSpace and Ingram Lightning Source. If you are not going to publish your book as a paperback, just skip the rest of this chapter and move to the next chapter on publishing your book as an eBook.

❏ **Publish Your Paperback at CreateSpace**

If you have followed the steps in the previous chapters about preparing your files for publishing your book as a paperback, the actual process of uploading these files for publication is relatively simple and straightforward. The first place you can upload the files to is CreateSpace. This is the paperback publishing arm of Amazon, and may be the only place

If your book is popular enough that you will be printing a million copies, you probably want to find a professional distribution company to do the work of printing and distributing your book for you.

you choose to publish your paperback. Using their publishing platform, you can print one book at a time, or a million. Of course, if your book is popular enough that you will be printing a million copies, you probably want to find a professional distribution company to do the work of printing and distributing your book for you. Assuming, however, that you will only be printing a few copies at a time (or a few hundred), CreateSpace is the way to go.

There are a few things to keep in mind before you get started. It is free to set up your book for printing through CreateSpace, but there are various "upsell" options which you can purchase as you go through. You need to decide which of these options best fit your needs and budget. I will explain a few of these options as we go through and what I usually do, but you must decide for yourself what your budget can afford. So let us begin. First, you must login at CreateSpace, or create an account if you have not yet done so.

Once you login, click the "Add New Title" link. The process of creating your book is pretty self-explanatory. CreateSpace takes you step-by-step through the process of adding the title of the book and choosing the various options needed for publication. On the first screen, where it asks for the name of the project, this is not the book title yet, but simply a name that identifies your project. I typically use my book title for this name.

I highly recommend that the first few times you publish on CreateSpace, you use the Guided process.

Then choose whether you want the Guided or the Expert setup process. I highly recommend that the first few times you publish on CreateSpace, you use the Guided process. Later, once you get familiar with the files that CreateSpace needs, you can use the Expert process if you desire. For this book, I will use the Guided process.

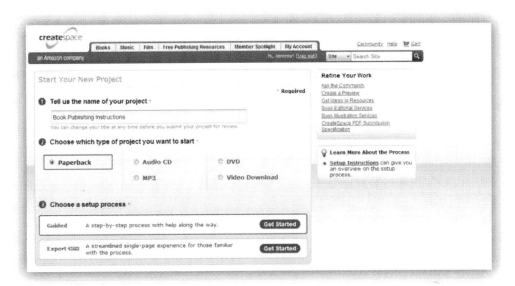

On the next screen, you are asked to enter the Title, the Subtitle (if you have one), the primary author and any other contributors, as well as the series, edition, language, and publication date. Enter as much information as you can and click "Save & Continue." If there are any errors, CreateSpace will tell you what needs to be fixed.

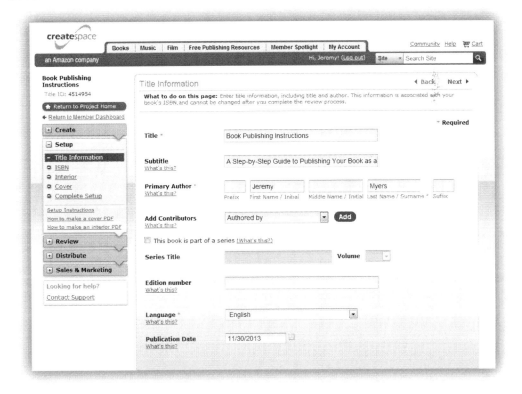

You are now asked to enter your ISBN number. Here is one of the first places you can pay a little bit of money for some CreateSpace options. Printing a paperback book requires an ISBN number. CreateSpace will give you one for free, but this requires you to list CreateSpace as your publisher. If you are fine with that, then go ahead and choose this option. If, however, you have your own publishing company, you can also buy an ISBN from CreateSpace for only $10, and list your imprint as the publisher. For my books, I purchased ISBNs from Bowker Identifier Services since I buy them in bulk and get them for cheaper than $10 each. So I choose the "Provide Your Own ISBN' option, and enter the requested information. I use the ISBN number I have reserved for the paperback edition of my book and enter the name of my publishing company.

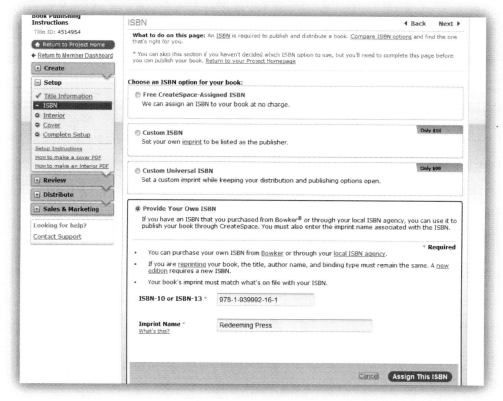

The next step is to set up the interior pages of your book. You need to select whether your book is black and white or color print, what kind of paper you will use, and the trim size of your book. I usually choose a black and white interior with white paper. The trim size is the size of the paper you chose back in the Page Layout section of the Preparing for Publication chapter of this book. I usually print my books at 5.5 x 8.5, but this current book is a bit larger, at 7 x 10. Then I choose to upload my book file, and I upload the PDF which was created in an earlier step of preparing for publication. While you can upload other formats than the PDF, this file format provides you with the most control over how your final book appears in print. Note also that since I do not design my interior pages to include "bleed" I select the option which shows no bleed on my pages. Probably the only time you would want to select the option with bleed is when you have interior images or background colors that bleed off the edge of the page, just as you did with the paperback cover image in a previous chapter.

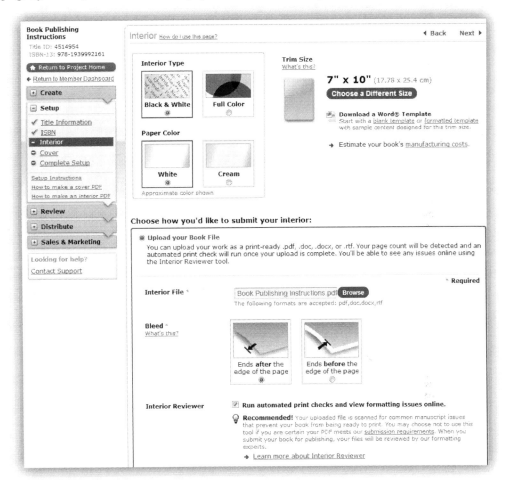

Once you click "Save" the PDF file will upload to CreateSpace and will get processed. If you selected the "automated print check" option (which you should), it will also check the file for any potential issues that might be encountered in the printing process. Once this print check is done, you can use the online Interior Reviewer tool to see how your paperback book will look in print. If any issues were found with the file you uploaded, the Interior Reviewer will show you what and where these issues are.

As can be seen in the following screenshot, the Interior Reviewer found a few problems with my file. It says that some of my images are less than 200 dpi, and they highly recommend that all images be at least 300 dpi. Due to the nature of which images it was warning me about, there was little I could do to fix this, so ignored this warning and hoped that it didn't look too bad in print. If you are reading this book as a paperback, I will let you be the judge of the image quality.

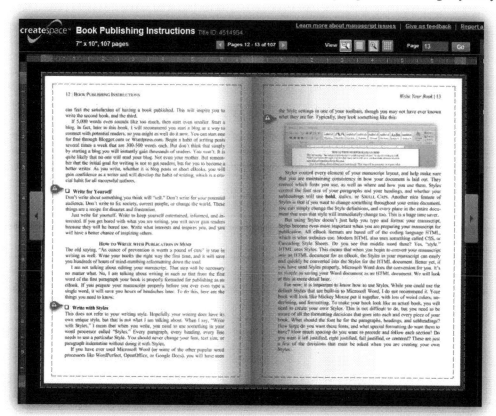

I highly recommend you look through most of the pages of your book to make sure it appears the way you want. While you can order a paper proof of your book at a later step, this step here is equivalent to viewing a digital proof of your paperback book. If you find issues and fix them in your Word document, you then have to create a new PDF and upload it to CreateSpace and then launch the Interior Reviewer again. If there are issues with your book that do not need fixing, you can press the "Skip Interior Reviewer" link to go to the next step.

> *I highly recommend you look through most of the pages of your book to make sure it appears the way you want.*

The next step is to upload the PDF of your cover, which you created in the "Create a Cover" chapter. Remember to upload the paperback version of your cover, rather than the eBook version. The paperback version should have a spine and a back cover along with the front cover image, and the entire cover will be surrounded by image bleed. When you get to the step of uploading your cover to

CreateSpace, you will be given a choice between Matte and Glossy finish. This really is personal preference, but I always choose Glossy. Select the "Upload a Print-Ready PDF Cover" option near the bottom, and then browse to the file location on your computer for this file.

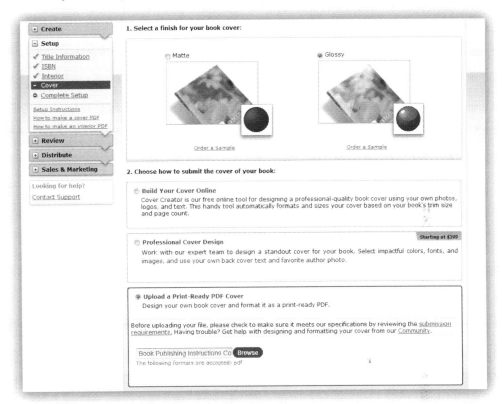

Once you are done with this step, you will see one final screen to check your files and book details. If anything needs changing, feel free to edit it. If everything looks good, click the "Submit Files for Review" button at the bottom of the screen. The files will then be reviewed by someone at Amazon. If there are any issues that need to be addressed or corrections that need to be made, they will let you know via email. If they accept your book as ready to print, they will give you the option of purchasing a paperback proof of your book. This is probably something you should do, as this will show you exactly what the final print version of your book will look like. If there are issues with the cover or interior pages, you want to know about it before people start buying your book.

If there are issues with the cover or interior pages, you want to know about it before people start buying your book.

While you wait for Amazon to approve your files for printing, and while you wait for your paper proof to arrive in the mail, you can set up the Distribution options that are available through Amazon. On the CreateSpace sidebar, click the "Distribute" tab and select "Channels." In the available options, I select all that are available to me. Amazon used to charge $25 for Expanded Distribution, but they have recently made these additional options available for free. Even at $25, it was a good deal, as it made your paperback book available to Bookstores and Online Retailers and through CreateSpace Direct. I think they made it free due to increasing competition in the publishing industry. Note that your paperback book is not eligible for distribution to Libraries and Academic Institutions because you do not have a CreateSpace-assigned ISBN number. This is the one drawback to using your own ISBN number, but the benefits outweigh this one drawback. Besides, Libraries and Academic Institutions can still purchase and stock your book through the regular distribution channels.

> *Your book is not eligible for distribution to Libraries and Academic Institutions because you do not have a CreateSpace-assigned ISBN number.*

On the next screen, you can set the pricing for your paperback book. There are no set rules on pricing your book. You want to price the book low enough so that it will be bought, but you also need to set a price that will cover your time and expense of writing and printing the book. Amazon CreateSpace will show you what the minimum price is for your book. Even if you set this minimum price, you will still earn about a 20% royalty on the book. The higher you set your price, the greater your royalty payment will be. Of course, if

Even if you set this minimum price, you will still earn about a 20% royalty on the book. The higher you set your price, the greater your royalty payment will be.

you set it too high, nobody will buy your book and you won't make any money. Go to this page to learn more about <u>how royalties are calculated</u>. I am not fully sure yet how I will price this book, but I put in a temporary price of $14.99, and will adjust it later.

The next step is to select the cover finish, which was already done in the "Setup" section, and I don't know why Amazon asks for it again. So move on to the "Description" section. This is where you will enter the description you wrote when you created the Book Information Document earlier. Just copy and paste your book description into the box, select the BISAC category, enter your Author Biography, the Book Language, Country of Publication, and the Search Keywords (no more than 5). Once you are done, click "Save and Continue."

The next screen invites you to publish your book on the Kindle. You do not need to do this, since the files that CreateSpace sends over to the Amazon Kindle Direct Publishing program are not the ideal files to be using for publishing on KDP. You will be uploading your own files made specifically for the Amazon Kindle in the next chapter. So just ignore this invitation, and wait for your book to be approved for sale on Amazon through CreateSpace.

Once you get the confirmation email and you have reviewed your proof for printing errors, you have successfully published your paperback book! Congratulations, you are now a published author, and your book is available online in the largest bookstore in the world!

However, to reach the widest number of people possible, there is another place you might want to publish your paperback book.

❑ Publish Your Paperback at Lightning Source

If you publish your book as a paperback through Amazon CreateSpace, you do not really need to publish your book through Ingram's Lightning Source. As a result, I typically do not publish any of my books through Lightning Source. There are, however, some benefits to publishing through Lightning Source which you might desire for your book. Below is a description of the pros and cons. (Go here to see an info graphic on some of these pros and cons, but note that this image is somewhat dated and all the details are no longer accurate.)

First, if you want your book to be printed as a hardback, you will need to print with Ingram's Lightning Source. CreateSpace does not offer this option. Second, the print quality of Lightning Source tends to be a bit better than that of CreateSpace, though most readers will not be able to tell the difference. Third, since publishing through Lightning Source requires you to have an actual publishing company and your own ISBN number, it is much easier to get your book onto the shelves of bookstores and into book catalogs when you publish through Lightning Source. Fourth, while CreateSpace sets most wholesale discounts at 20%, Lightning Source allows the publisher to set the wholesale discount. If you set it at the industry standard of 40%, this will encourage more bookstores to stock your book. Fifth, remember how CreateSpace would not allow you the option of distributing your book to Libraries and Academic Institutions unless you used a "CreateSpace-assigned ISBN"? Well, Ingram Lightning Source makes your book available to their network of 38,000 retail and library partners around the world. Finally, Lightning Source allows bookstores to return unsold copies of your book, which is a great incentive for bookstores to stock your book in the first place. Most bookstores will not stock books that cannot be returned.

Now, while all this sounds great, there are some pretty serious drawbacks to publishing with Lightning Source which you also need to be aware of. First, you absolutely need to have your own publishing label set up and your own ISBN numbers to publish with Lightning Source. If you don't have these, you have no options; you must stick with CreateSpace. Second, while the setup at CreateSpace is free, Lightning Source will cost at least $50. Third, the printing cost for a book is a bit higher at Lightning Source than at CreateSpace. Fourth, although bookstores will not stock books that cannot be returned, if they return books to Lightning Source, you, as the publisher, have to reimburse Lightning Source for the returned books, plus pay a processing fee per book. This can add up to a huge amount of money quite quickly. You can, of course, tell Lightning Source to not accept returns, but then bookstores will likely not agree to stock your book.

So what is the best way to proceed? For most self-published authors, publishing through CreateSpace will be adequate. If, however, you think that publishing your book through Ingram's Lightning Source is something that fits within your publishing goals and needs, then follow the guide below. Note that Ingram has created their own free guide as well which I highly recommend if you are going to use their publishing platform.

The first thing to do is note that the small and independent publishing arm of Lightning Source is called Ingram Spark. Just as Amazon uses CreateSpace, Ingram Lightning Source uses Ingram Spark. While larger and more established publishers can use Lightning Source directly, smaller publishers can use Ingram Spark to print titles and fulfills orders placed through any of their 38,000 retail and library partners around the world. Ingram Spark also gets your eBooks listed on major online retail sites, including iBooks, Barnes & Noble, and Kindle. Better still, the setup costs are potentially lower than going through Lightning Source directly while the features are nearly identical.

Begin by going to Ingram Spark and creating an account. You will have to digitally sign some legal documents and set up some security questions, but all of that is pretty standard. Once you have created the account, you are taken to the publishing screen which appears to be almost identical to that of CreateSpace. To get started, simply click the "Add a New Title" button.

You will then be given the option to publish your book as a print book only, as an eBook only, or as both. Choose the option that fits your publishing needs, and then enter the details that Ingram Spark requests. For this guide, I will publish both.

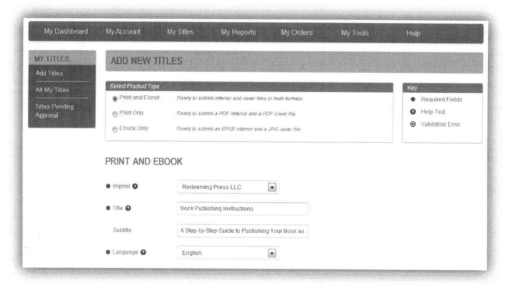

On the next screen, you enter the author, the BISAC categories, and the book description. All of this can be pulled from the Book Information Document which you created earlier. One of the things I really love about Ingram Spark on this screen is their "Search" feature for the BISAC categories. If you click the "Find Subjects" button, a screen opens up which allows you to use the keywords from your Book Information Document to search for the best BISAC categories.

As you can see by the screenshot below, I found two additional categories which I did not have listed in my Book Information Document earlier.

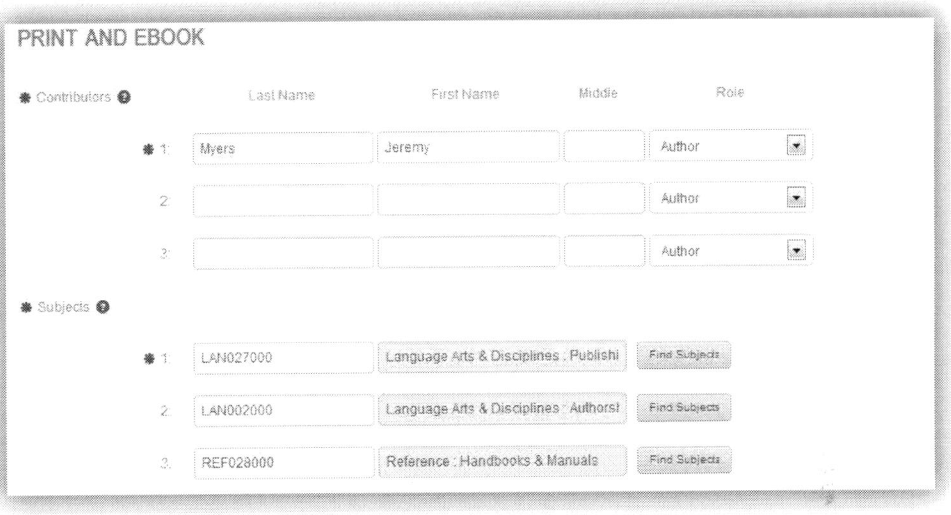

On the next screen, you are asked to choose the various printing options for your paperback book. The trim size and page count for your book will determine which binding types are available to you. So pick the trim size first, and then enter the page count for your book. Choose from the available options that are left for the interior type, binding type, paper type, and laminate type. If you have questions on the binding type, case laminate is a hardcover book, cloth bound is also hardbound, but uses a cloth-textured cover. Perfect bound is a paperback book, and saddle stitch is for books with less than 32 pages. With saddle stitch, they print the pages of your book, fold them in half, and then staple them on the edge. They do not have spines. You can see in the following image what I have chosen for this book.

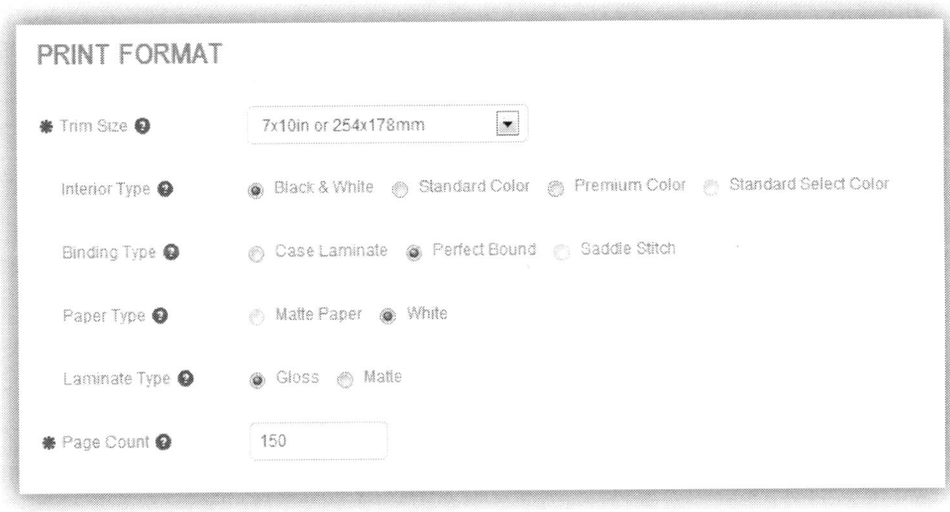

The next screen asks for the ISBN number and pricing for the print version of your book. This is also where you are given the option to accept returns on your book. You learned earlier in this chapter about the pros and cons of making your book returnable. I recommend that unless you are certain your book will sell tens of thousands of copies, you do not make your book returnable. Otherwise, some bookstore may purchase 10 copies, sell none of them, and then want to return them at your expense. If you do choose to allow book returns, you have the option of paying for Ingram to ship the unsold copies to you at your expense, or to have Ingram destroy the returned copies. Either way, you will still have to pay for the wholesale cost of the books that are returned, plus a processing fee. This screen also asks you to set prices for other markets around the world. Use the Google monetary converter to figure out what the price for these other markets should be.

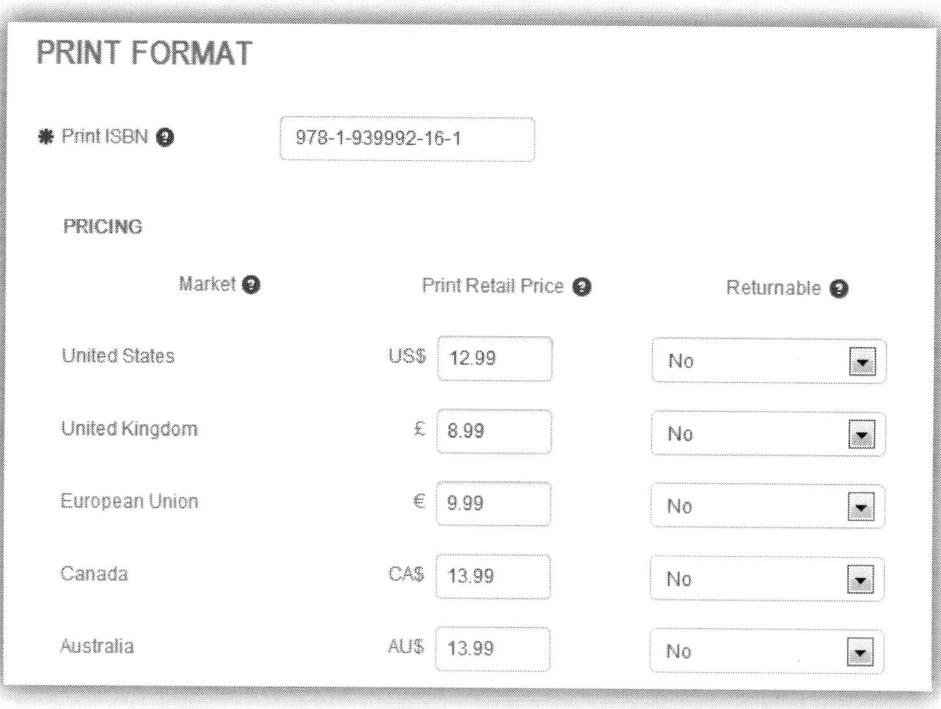

PRINT FORMAT

✳ Print ISBN ❓   978-1-939992-16-1

PRICING

Market ❓	Print Retail Price ❓		Returnable ❓	
United States	US$	12.99	No	▾
United Kingdom	£	8.99	No	▾
European Union	€	9.99	No	▾
Canada	CA$	13.99	No	▾
Australia	AU$	13.99	No	▾

The next screen asks for all the same details as for the paperback edition, but this time for the eBook editions. It asks for two sets of prices, one for the regular eBook price, and one for Apple. The only difference between the two is that Apple requires book prices to end in ".99." Since I am already following this practice, I keep both sets of prices the same. One strange thing about this screen is that it asks for the page count. Since eBooks don't really have page counts, I am not sure why they ask for this, but I entered the same number as I gave for the paperback. Note, of course, that since I am writing this book while I upload it (how else can I get the screen shots?), my final page count for this book might be slightly higher or lower than what I am reporting. I will have to come back and change these numbers when the book is finished.

EBOOK FORMAT

✱ Ebook ISBN ❷   978-1-939992-18-5

PRICING

Currencies ❷	Ebook Retail Price ❷	Apple Ebook (Agency) Price ❷
US Dollars	US$ 9.99	US$ 9.99
British Pounds	£ 8.99	£ 8.99
Euros	€ 8.99	€ 8.99
CA Dollars	CA$ 10.99	CA$ 10.99
AU Dollars	AU$ 10.99	AU$ 10.99

✱ Publication Date ❷   11/30/2013

✱ On Sale Date ❷   11/30/2013

✱ Page Count ❷   150

The final screen simply asks if you have the legal right to sell eBooks anywhere in the world. I do, so I selected Yes.

Now that you have finished setting up your title, you will begin the process of uploading the necessary files for creating the paperback book and the eBook at Ingram. The process is quite simple. You can drag and drop files from your computer, or choose a file to upload them. Once uploaded, the files get deposited in a section of the screen for "Uploaded Files" and you can drag and drop them to the appropriate places on your screen.

Note that for the eBook edition of your book, Ingram Spark requires an ePub document. So far, you have not created one of these, but will do so in the next chapter. This current chapter, of course, is only focused on publishing your book as a paperback book, and so from this point on, the steps for publishing your eBook at Ingram will not be discussed. I prefer to publish my eBooks myself at the various websites that allow it, rather than have Ingram Spark do it for me. I can get better royalty payments from the various platforms by dealing with them directly than by allowing Ingram to serve as a middleman between myself and eBook publishing platforms like Apple iBooks and Barnes & Noble.

For the print edition of your book, you need to upload the PDF file which was created earlier, and the PDF cover file which contains not only the front cover of the book, but the spine and back cover as well. But you cannot simply use the same cover that was used for CreateSpace. Why not? Because CreateSpace and Ingram Spark use different paper, and the thickness on this paper requires you to adjust your spine thickness to fit the Ingram Spark requirements. To find out what specifications for printing with Ingram Spark, access the Ingram Spark File Creation Guide. Also, as mentioned earlier in this book, you can use the Lightning Source spine width calculator to figure out the thickness for your spine. Make sure you use the exact same settings you entered for the paperback edition of your book.

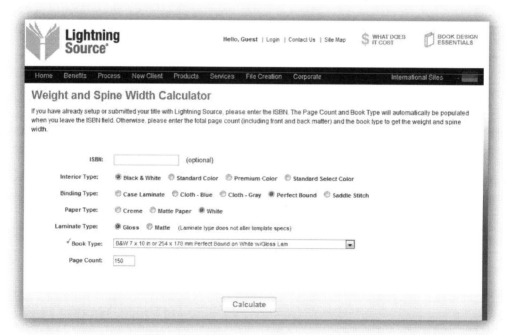

When I calculated my spine width, it gave me a width of 0.321 inches. Using the exact same page count, CreateSpace told me my spine width was 0.3378 inches. The difference is not a huge amount, but it is enough to make a difference in how the spine looks on your book. This difference will be even more exaggerated with a higher page count.

So before you upload your cover file, you need to return to Adobe Photoshop and edit your cover file so that it has the proper spine size. If you saved your cover document as a .psd file with all the layers and guides intact, this minor adjustment will not take long. Of course, just as I did not show how to create the Adobe Photoshop file, I am also not going to show how to edit it. That process is too involved for this publishing guide. Once the edit is finished and you have a new cover file saved as a PDF, return to Ingram Spark to upload this new cover file. In the following screen shot, you can see that I have uploaded the necessary files and then dragged and dropped them into the proper locations for the print book files.

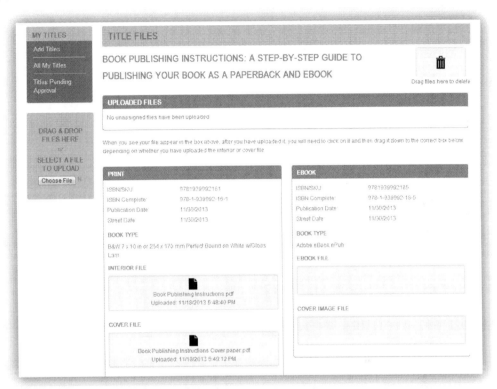

Once you submit your book, a screen will open which will validate your files. There may be some errors that need correcting, and if so, these errors usually have something to do with the images in your PDF or whether or not the fonts were properly embedded. Sometimes, if you are printing a black and white book but the PDF has color images, Ingram Spark will ask you to convert images in the book to CMYK color instead of RGB, convert the PDF to a grayscale document, flatten all the images, embed any fonts, and a variety of other items. As mentioned earlier when the PDF was originally created, all of these corrections can be done within the Print Production Preflight section of Adobe Acrobat. There are a wide variety of errors which can be produced, and you simply need to do your best to resolve these errors as best you can before moving on to the next step. If there is something you do not know how to do, search Google for tips and suggestions.

On this current book, due to the way I inserted and compressed the images into the Word document, I was told that my image quality was too low. Lightning Source recommends black and white images to be 300 dpi and color images to be at least 600 dpi. Due to Microsoft Word's image compression feature, most of my images are around 220 dpi, with many being only 96 dpi.

Here is the warning that Ingram Spark gave me:

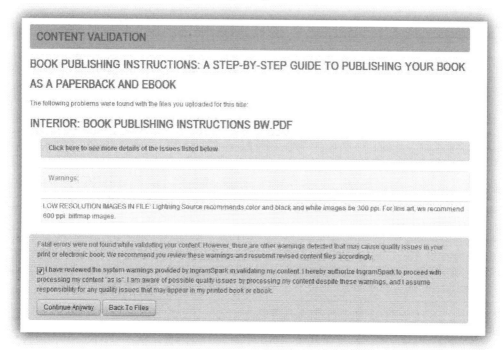

After everything is approved, you will be taken to the Title Submission screen where you have to pay Ingram Spark for the Cover Setup, Book Block Setup, and the Print on Demand Access Fee. Once you pay the fees, your book will enter the final approval process, and just as with CreateSpace, you will get an email once your book has been approved and is available for purchase.

This is where the guide concludes for publishing your book at Ingram Spark for the Lightning Source publishing platform and Ingram distribution channels.

Now that you have published your paperback books on Amazon and maybe on Lightning Source as well, you are ready turn to the process of publishing your book as an eBook. This is the subject of the next chapter.

PUBLISH YOUR eBOOK

The popularity of eBooks is on the rise, so whether you publish your book as a paperback or not, you must publish your book as an eBook. In fact, depending on your publishing goals and the length of your book, you may want to publish your book *only* as an eBook. As I mentioned earlier in this book, if the total word count of your book is less than 30,000 words, you probably do not want to publish your book as a paperback and should stick with just eBook versions.

In this chapter you will learn to publish your eBook on a variety of platforms, including Amazon, Barnes & Noble, Google, Apple, and Smashwords. I will also provide you with instructions for publishing your eBook on your own website or blog. Obviously, you do not need to publish your book on all of these sites, and may choose to only publish on one or two. I recommend that you at least publish on Amazon, since they are the largest bookseller in the world, and as a second choice, publish your eBook on Smashwords, since they can distribute your book to Barnes & Noble, Apple iBooks, and several other booksellers as well. Ultimately, of course, your publishing goals and available time determine where and how you distribute your eBook.

❑ **Publish Your eBook at Amazon**
The first location where you should consider publishing your eBook is Amazon, through their Kindle Direct Publishing (KDP) platform. Depending on what you want to do with your book, Amazon may also be the *only* place you initially publish your eBook. I will explain why in the next chapter on Marketing your Book, but for now, let me just say that there are numerous benefits to publishing your book exclusively on Amazon for at least the first three months. My personal pattern is to first list my eBook on Amazon for at least three months. When those months are completed, I then publish it on my own website, Redeeming Press, as well as on Barnes & Noble, Google Books, Apple iBooks, and Smashwords. The paperback editions, however, are available during this entire time through Amazon <u>CreateSpace</u> and Ingram Lightning Source (if I use Ingram). Follow the following guide to publish your eBook with Amazon. Note that Amazon has <u>created their own guide as well</u> which I highly recommend.

To publish on Amazon's KDP platform, you must first login at to the Kindle Direct Publishing platform at kdp.amazon.com. Obviously, if you do not have a KDP account, you will need to create on first. Once you have logged in, you will be taken directly to the KDP publishing dashboard. My dashboard shows some of the books I have already published. To get started publishing your book, simply click the "Add new title" button.

The KDP platform is quite simple to use. The first screen is where you enter all the details about your book from the Book Information Data document you created earlier and also upload your book cover and manuscript. There are good descriptions with each one of the items, but let me explain a few of the steps in more detail.

First, you are given the option to enroll in KDP Select. There are many benefits to doing so, which are listed on the screen. However, the one drawback is that Amazon prohibits you from listing the book in digital format on any other platform during the entire three months. This means that if you enroll in KDP Select, you cannot publish the book on Barnes & Noble, on Apple iBooks, or on any other website. I usually enroll my books in KDP select for the first three months of publication. I explain why in the next chapter on "Marketing Your Book."

Next, enter all the information that is requested. Just as with the book title in the paperback editions above, when it asks for the Book name, type in the book name, followed by a colon, and then the subtitle of the book. If you look at books on Amazon, you can see that this is how it is usually done. Following the Book name, include the Publisher, the Description, the Book contributor (yourself as the author), the Language, Publication date, and ISBN. Make ·sure that you use the ISBN reserved for the Mobi edition of the book.

Following this, verify that you hold the necessary publishing rights to the book, and enter the categories and keywords which you have decided on. This process on KDP might also enable you to refine and edit the keywords you have selected. If you find any additional keywords, make sure you add them to your Book Information Document as they will come in handy later.

Finally, you need to upload your Book Cover and your Book File. Since this is an eBook edition of the book, make sure you upload the eBook version of your book cover. This version will not have the spine or the back cover, but will only be an image of the front cover.

As for the book file you upload, this depends on which file format you created. If you chose not to create the HTML file, then upload the Word document. If you upload the Word document, and the preview of the book looks fine, then you are done. If, however, the book looks a little strange in places, then you will need to upload the HTML file (or the Zip file if your book has images). If you chose not to create an HTML file and you now think you need one, you will need to go back to the chapter on formatting the eBook and follow the steps listed there. Whatever you do, don't upload the PDF. The formatting really gets messed up when the KDP platform tries to work with the PDF book format.

Since I created an HTML file for this book (and then Zipped it up with the image files), that is what I will upload to Amazon. I also check the option to Enable Digital Rights management, as this option keeps my book from getting shared illegally.

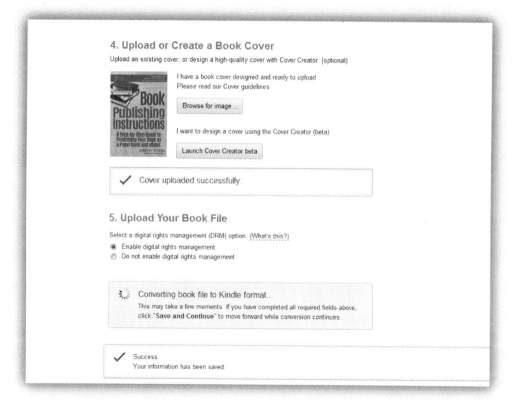

Once the file uploads and gets converted to Kindle format, you will get an "Upload and Conversion successful" message. Underneath you can now preview your eBook to see how it will look on a Kindle. I highly recommend you preview every page of the book to look for any strange formatting issues. If you see any, go fix them in your file, and then upload the Word document again, or convert it to the HTML file for uploading.

If you are happy with the way your book appears on the various Kindle platforms, go on to Step 2: Rights & Pricing. Here is where you select the publishing rights and the pricing for your eBook. I always select Worldwide rights, and price my eBook a few dollars less than the price I set for the paperback copies. There is no rule to what price works best. I have seen some authors sell thousands of copies of a book at $39.99, while other authors can hardly sell ten books at $0.99. You choose a price which works best for you. One thing to note, however, is that KDP has two royalty structures, one at 35% and one at 70%. If you want to choose the 70% royalty, you must price your book at $2.99 or more. I am going to set this eBook price at $7.99, though this may change by the time the book is published.

> *I have seen some authors sell thousands of copies of a book at $39.99, while other authors can hardly sell ten books at $0.99.*

Near the bottom, I also enroll the book in the Kindle MatchBook program and allow Kindle Book Lending. Both of these provide the opportunity for my book to get into the hands of more people, which is always a good idea.

Kindle Matchbook is only helpful if you are also going to be publishing your book as a paperback. Essentially what it does is allow the person to buy your eBook at a discounted rate if they have already bought the paperback version. In other words, if they buy your paperback book, say for $12.99, and your eBook is usually priced at $7.99, Amazon will give them the option of buying your eBook at the discounted MatchBook price that you set on this screen. I enable it on all the books I sell through Amazon since it is a good way to encourage people to buy both the paperback and the eBook versions of book if they are available.

Once you have entered all the details and uploaded your book, simply check that little box which says that you hold the necessary rights to publish your book, and then click the "Save and Publish" button. Someone at Amazon reviews your files and double-checks the file format of your manuscript, and you will usually receive an email notification within 24 hours (but it can take longer) about the status of your book.

One thing that Amazon is going to do during this process is make sure that your book is not found anywhere else on the internet if you have opted to participate in the KDP Select program. Again, by joining the KDP Select program, you have agreed to give Amazon the exclusive rights to publish your book for three months. Don't try to trick the system. Be honest. Amazon is quite good at finding your book if it is listed elsewhere, and if they find it for sale on another site, this will drastically slow down your publishing process at KDP and may even prohibit you from joining the KDP Select program.

For example, I have a practice of blogging heavily about my books before I publish them. In fact, with some of my books, as much as 70% of the manuscript might be posted in the form of blog posts before the book gets published. Invariably, Amazon discovers that I have done this, and sends me an email asking about the content of these posts, and also asking me to verify that I have not simply stolen someone else's blog posts to make a book. Remember, they also want to make sure I own the publishing rights. They want to make sure I have not plagiarized someone else's blog posts and published them as my own book. When I get an email from Amazon enquiring about the content of the book online, I usually reply with this email in response:

> The title of the book in question is "BOOK TITLE HERE." As it has not yet been published, it does not have an Amazon ID.
>
> The content of this book is available only on my own website. Here, for example, is the landing page for the book, which contains links to much of the content in this book:
>
> WEB LINKS HERE
>
> I am the sole owner of the copyrighted material in this book, and though I have posted the book online on my blog, it is not public domain material. I am the sole author and owner of this material. I control the exclusive rights to this book. I carefully read the KDP content guidelines (https://kdp.amazon.com/self-publishing/help?topicId=A2TOZW0SV7IR1U) and it clearly states that Amazon will not accept content that is freely available on the web unless I am the copyright owner of the content. As I am the sole copyright owner of the content, this book qualifies for being published on KDP.
>
> To answer your second question as to why the content is available online, I believe this is the future of publishing. I gain interest in my books by writing them online, getting feedback, comments, and suggestions from my readers. I then edit and update all the chapters based on the feedback and input I receive, and publish the book on KDP. This not only helps my readers feel more involved in the writing process, but gets them interested in buying and reading the final edition when it is published. Publishing books in this way helps generate interest and sales.
>
> I look forward to making this book available to my reading audience.
>
> Jeremy Myers

So far, sending an email such as this one has not hindered my ability to publish books through Kindle Direct Publishing, nor has it hindered my ability to join the KDP Select program.

Once you receive notification that your book has been published, you can then go into the KDP website and schedule the five days to give it away for free, or schedule the Kindle Countdown feature if you are going to use it (see the next chapter on book marketing for more on these topics).

Of course, you want to reach as many markets as you can, and have your book in as many formats as possible, and so the rest of this chapter will show you how to publish your book on various other websites and in various other formats. The process for publishing your book elsewhere is quite similar to what you have just completed on Amazon, and so I will include fewer details and explanations than I have for the Amazon publishing process.

Just remember that if you choose to participate in KDP Select, you cannot publish your book electronically on these other sites for at least three months. This only applies to the digital versions. You can have paperback editions available elsewhere during these three months. But while you are waiting, you can still upload the files and prepare for publication on these other websites, so that once the three months have expired all you need to do is hit the "publish" button and you will be good to go.

> *Just remember that if you choose to participate in KDP Select, you cannot publish your book electronically on these other sites for at least three months.*

One thing you can do during these three months is to link your paperback and eBook versions of your book on Amazon. Though Amazon might usually do this automatically within two weeks, I have found that it helps to alert Amazon that you have two different versions of the book for sale on their website, and they will link them together so that when people look for your book, they are given the option of purchasing it as either a paperback or eBook.

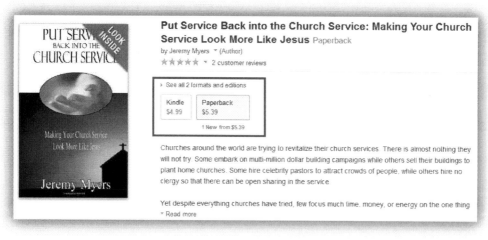

To speed up this process of linking your books, start in your Amazon KDP account, and click the "Contact Us" link. You will be presented with some menu options for what sort of question you want to ask. Select the "Product Page" option, and from there, choose the "Linking Print and Kindle Editions" item from the submenu. Provide the information that they ask for, which is primarily the

Amazon ASIN of the Kindle edition and the ISBN of the print edition. Amazon will usually get back to you within 24 hours that this has been completed.

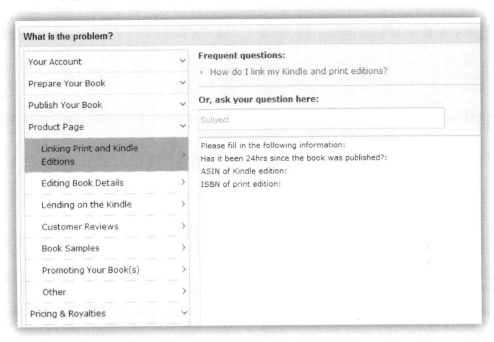

❏ **Publishing Your eBook on Your Website or Blog**

If you have a blog or website with a shopping cart, you may want to list your books for sale through you own website. Again, if you are using KDP Select on Amazon, you cannot even list your books for sale on your own website (or give them away for free). But once you opt out of KDP Select, and the 90 days are completed, one place you might want to list your books for sale is on you own website or blog. If you want a shopping cart, I highly recommend the <u>Wordpress eStore from Tips and Tricks HQ</u>. For my own site, I sell the PDF, Mobi, and ePub versions of the eBook so that people can buy whatever format works best for their particular eReader.

> *If you have a blog or website with a shopping cart, you may want to list your books for sale through you own website.*

To create your own eBook files to upload and distribute through your own website, you can use a free program called Calibre. You can download it for free at <u>calibre-ebook.com</u>. After you download and launch Calibre, you can use either the Microsoft Word document of your manuscript, or the HTML file you might have developed earlier to create books in the ePub and Mobi file types.

If you try to create the ePub file with your Word document, it is highly unlikely that it will validate properly.

Note, however, that if you try to create the ePub files with your Word document, it is highly unlikely that it will validate properly, which means that you need to go back to the chapter on formatting your eBook so that you can create the HTML file from which you will format the ePub file. If you are going to publishing on Google Books or Apple iBooks, you will absolutely need this ePub file anyway. On the other hand, if you don't want to sell books on your own website, or if you don't need the ePub file for Google and Apple iBooks, then you can probably ignore this section.

Once you have downloaded and installed the Calibre eBook management software, go ahead and open it up to get started. To add a book to Calibre, begin by simply clicking the "Add books" button in the upper left.

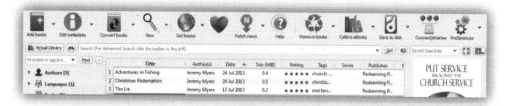

A screen will open, allowing you to search for your book file. You can add a book by selecting the same book file that you uploaded to Amazon KDP. If your book does not contain interior images, select the HTML file. If your book does contain interior images, select the Zip file. Once you have done this, Calibre will add the book to your library in whatever format you uploaded it in.

Once the book is in your Calibre program, the next thing to do is edit the metadata for the book. The metadata for a book is the description and keywords and other such details which help computer programs and websites know what your book is about so that people who search for your book can find it. To edit the metadata, simply click the "Edit metadata" button, and enter the information requested by Calibre. Most of the details can be pulled from the Book Information Document which you prepared earlier. The "Tags" are you keywords and key phrases. The "Ids" are for your ISBN number. You can only enter one ISBN, and so choose the one for the ePub file. If you uploaded your book already to Amazon KDP, you can also enter a second Id here for the Mobi file by using the Amazon-assigned ASIN number. You can enter both numbers in the "Ids" section this way:

```
isbn:9781939992185, amazon:B008B8PZVW
```

This is also on this screen that you can add the cover image for your book. Simply click the "Browse" button where it says "Change cover" to find the eBook cover which you created earlier. This is the same eBook cover you uploaded to Amazon KDP.

Over in the comments section, you can put in the Book Description from your Book Information Document. It is in this field that I also enter the other ISBN numbers that are reserved for this book. Note that if you know a bit of HTML, you can edit your Comments in HTML if you prefer by using the "HTML Source" tab at the bottom. My HTML code looks like this:

```
<div>

<p>Get your book published this year! Use this step-
by-step guide of book publishing instructions to turn
```

```
your unpublished manuscript into a paperback book or
an eBook for the Kindle, Nook, or iPad.</p>

<p>Detailed descriptions of what to do are accompa-
nied by screenshots for each step. Additional tools,
tips, and websites are also provided which will help
get your book published.</p>

<p>ISBN: 978-1-939992-16-1 (Paperback)</p>
<p>ISBN: 978-1-939992-17-8 (Mobi)</p>
<p>ISBN: 978-1-939992-18-5 (ePub)</p>

</div>
```

Here is what my Metadata screen looks like when everything has been added. After all the details have been entered, click the "OK" button at the bottom to be returned to the main Calibre book screen.

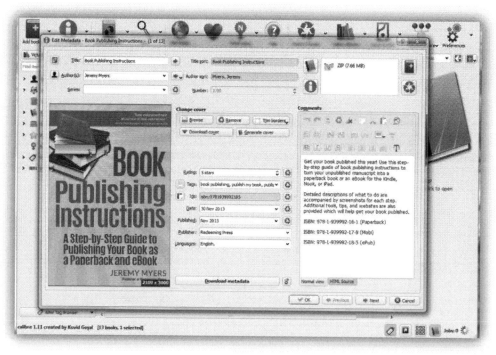

Once you are back in the main screen, it is time to convert your eBook to other file formats. You already have either the HTML format or the Zip format. You want to convert this to ePub and Mobi. To begin, click the "Convert books" button at the top of your screen. Another window will open up which allows you to convert your book to other formats using the little drop-down menu in the upper right-hand corner of the screen. Select the ePub option first.

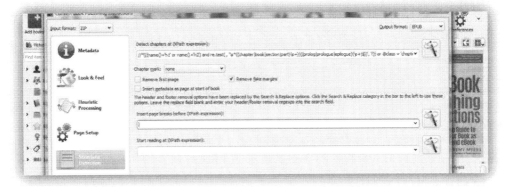

Before you hit "OK" at the bottom, you need to make a few minor adjustments to the options on the left. First, click the "Structure Detection" button. On the screen that appears, you need to make two changes. You must change the "Chapter mark" setting from "pagebreak" to "none." You have already entered chapter marks in your document through the use of HTML code, and have numerous page breaks throughout the document which do not indicate a new chapter, and so this setting would really mess up the layout and appearance of your eBook if you left it.

Second, delete the strange coding from the "Insert page breaks before" section. On my screen, it said this: //*[name()='h1' or name()='h2']. You don't want any of that, so just delete it all so the line is blank. You are done on this screen, but don't click "OK" yet. You still have some more settings to change.

The second setting to change is in the "Table of Contents" screen. Click that button on the left next. Again, you have already created a Table of Contents in your HTML file, and so you don't want Calibre to create another one. So what you need to do is put a checkmark in the box which says, "Do not add detected chapters to the Table of Contents" and then change all the numbers in the following fields to "0."

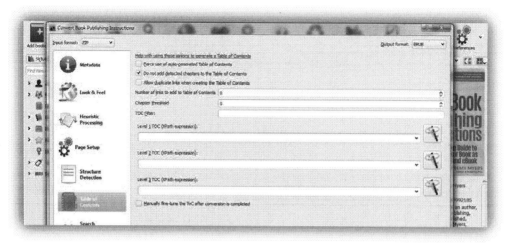

Third, you need to change a setting for the ePub output. Go to the ePub output settings, and select the "Do not split on page breaks" option.

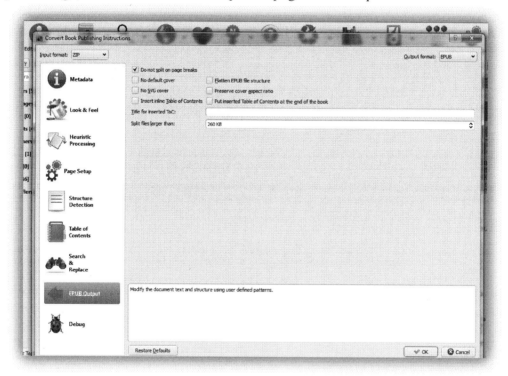

Once you have made these changes, you can now click "OK" at the bottom of the screen, and Calibre will convert the book to an ePub file. Once Calibre finishes, just repeat all the steps above again, except select "Mobi" from the dropdown menu on the right. Sometimes the Structure Detection and Table of Contents settings are remembered, and sometimes you have to enter them again. Either way, just double-check both to make sure.

When you are done, you will the various file formats listed on the right side of your book screen.

To find these files to upload to your website or to the other publishing platforms listed below, you can click the "Click to open" link next to "Path" to see the files. This is also the folder you will use if you need to edit any of your Calibre eBook files. How do you know if you need to edit them or not? Well, click on one of the file names to check the way it appears in a typical eBook reader. If anything looks strange, you may need to edit the file using Notepad++. How? I will explain briefly right after I show how to validate the ePub file.

One other note about Calibre: If you ever edit your book manuscript and need to upload new files, you will need to use the drop-down options in the "Remove books" button on the tool bar to remove certain file types, and the drop-down options in the "Add books" button to add the updated file types. You will also then need to re-create the various book formats according to the steps listed above.

Now, there is one last thing you need to do to the ePub file which you created. Your ePub file needs to be validated. Many eBook publishing sites will reject your file if it does not pass ePub validation. Before you do validation however, make sure that you have lots of free time on your hands, and are not having an overly stressful day. It is quite likely that somewhere along the way of validating your ePub file, you will want to curse your computer as well as any poor innocent soul standing nearby. If you are short on hair, the ePub validation process will likely make you lose what hair you have left. Any hair that doesn't fall out will likely turn grey or get torn out.

Having said that, I have tried my best to provide you with the step-by-step instructions for preparing your manuscript in a way that will avoid most of the ePub validation errors. If you followed the steps I provided in the chapters on writing your book and formatting your eBook, then it is possible that when you validate your ePub file, there will be no errors, and you can have a joyous celebration as you submit your files to Apple iBooks and the other sites that require the ePub file for publication.

So with these warnings in mind, begin by going to the <u>free online ePub validator</u> to upload your ePub file so that it can be checked for errors. Once there, browse to find your ePub file, upload it, and then click "validate" to run the test.

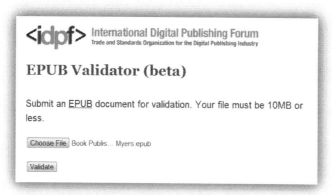

Note as well that the online ePub validator (at the time of writing) is using ePub Check version 2. If you want download the newest version of ePub Check, you can do so at <u>GitHub ePub Check page</u>. But since you need some technical know-how to actually install ePub Check 3 from GitHub, I recommend you stick with the online validator tool.

Once you run your ePub file through the ePub validator, you are going to get a lot of error messages that look like they were written by drunk monkeys. For example, I have seen these sorts of errors on my ePub files:

```
Length of the first filename in archive must be 8,
but was 22.
```

```
Item (___) exists in the zip file, but is not de-
clared in the OPF file
```

```
Irregular DOCTYPE: found '-//W3C//DTD XHTML 1.1
//EN', expecting '!DOCTYPE html PUBLIC "-//W3C//DTD
XHTML 1.1//EN" "http://www.w3.org/TR/xhtml11/DTD/
xhtml11.dtd
```

```
meta@dtb:uid content '' should conform to unique-
identifier in content.opf: '978-1-111111-11-1
```

You see? Error messages written by drunk monkeys. Thankfully, the eBook publishing world is rapidly evolving, and I believe that within a few years, publishing using the ePub format will become infinitely easier. Many of the errors above came from an earlier version of ePubCheck, but the more recent version, ePubCheck 3.0, has errors that are much more descriptive and helpful. Over time, the ePub standards will continue to evolve and become much more flexible and able to handle a wider variety of variations in coding and formatting.

Until then, the only suggestions I can really offer regarding any errors you might encounter is this: Google is your best friend. Whatever errors you see, copy them one by one into a Google search. You are not the first one to encounter this ePub validation error, and there are likely websites and forums out there where you can find out what the error means and how to fix it in your file. Here are a few of the sites I have found helpful as I try to fix and correct the validation errors on my own ePub files:

- How to Edit Your ePub eBook
- ePubCheck help page at Smashwords
- Google's ePub Fixer
- How to Create a Usable ePub file
- Six Tips for your ePub file

For my own ePub editing trials, I found that first link to be the most helpful. Once your ePub file validates without any errors, and once you like the appearance of it in Calibre, you are ready to upload it to the various sites that use it.

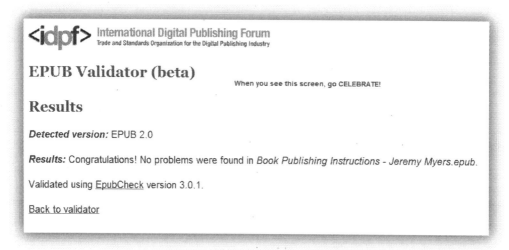

At this point, you could return to Ingram Spark and publish your book with them as an eBook. You would simply upload your ePub file and the eBook cover, and they would do the rest. They would then distribute your eBook to Barnes & Noble, Apple iBooks, and several other publishing platforms. However, the drawback is that since Ingram Spark is serving as the middleman between these various publishing platforms, they take a percentage of your royalty payments. So although it is more work, I prefer to deal with each publishing platform directly, than allow Ingram Spark to publish my eBook for me. The rest of this chapter will show you how to do this, beginning with Barnes & Noble.

❑ Publish Your eBook at Barnes & Noble

The publishing process at Barnes & Noble for their Nook eReader is similar to the publishing process at Amazon. First, go to the Nook Press website, create an account, and sign in. Once you have signed in, simply click the "Create new Project" button near the top to start the publishing process.

Just as with Amazon, there is a step-by-step process in which Nook Press will ask you for various details about your book, and you will upload the Microsoft Word document to see how it looks. If things look strange, you may need to go back to the chapter on formatting your eBook to create an HTML and ePub file.

You can upload the HTML file if your book does not have images, but if your book does have images, you will need to use the ePub file.

Since I have interior images and have already validated my ePub file, I upload this file format to Nook Press. After you upload the file, you can Preview the NOOK Book to see how it appears. Just as you checked the appearance of your ePub book with Calibre and your Mobi book with Amazon, I also recommend you check the appearance of your ePub book here with Barnes & Noble. If there weren't any problems on Calibre, there might not be any problems here either, but it never hurts to double check.

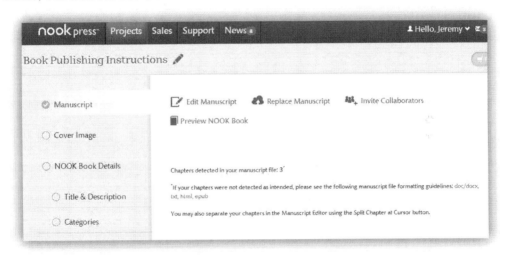

If you don't like the appearance of something, you can always try to upload the Word document, or if that doesn't work, you can edit the ePub files following the guides near the end of the previous section. For example, on this current eBook, I discovered that some of my subheadings looked a little small, and so I had to go un-Zip the ePub file and edit the stylesheet, and then Zip the ePub file back up and upload it to Barnes & Noble once again.

After you are satisfied with how your manuscript appears, you can go on to upload a cover image, and then add in all the book details, just as you have done at Amazon and with Calibre. I am not going to provide a detailed guide on this, because by now, the process should be pretty

After you are satisfied with how your manuscript appears, you can go on to upload a cover image and then add in all the book details.

familiar. Once everything is entered, click the green "Publish" button, and you will get a confirmation email when your files have been accepted and your book is available for purchase through Barnes & Noble.

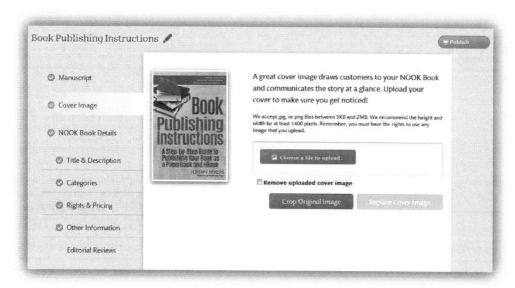

Note as well that if you want to publish your book at Barnes & Noble, but don't want to deal with their publishing platform, you can publish your book on Smashwords (instructions below), and they will send the eBook over to Barnes & Noble for you. I think they only take about 5% of your royalty payments for serving as the middleman, which is not a bad deal at all.

❑ **Publish Your eBook at Google Books**
Though few know about it, you can also publish your books with Google. Though the jury is still out on whether Google will expand their publishing platform into something that will rival Amazon or Apple, and though Google has a bad habit of starting services, letting them run for a few years, and then cancelling them, I think that Google Books will be around for the long haul.

To begin, go to Google Books Partner Center, and create an account.

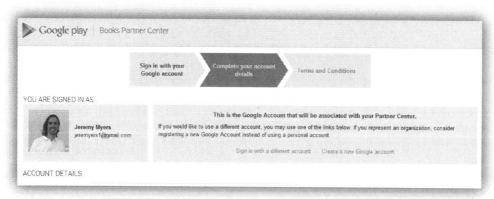

Once you are logged in, you will see your Book Catalog. Click the "Add books" button to get started. It will ask you for your ISBN number for the book, though this is optional with Google Books. If you opted to publish your book without an ISBN, simply check the box which says that you don't have an ISBN or other identifier for this book. After you have entered the ISBN, click the "Create" button.

On the next screen, enter all the details it asks for, most of which you should have on your Book Information Data page.

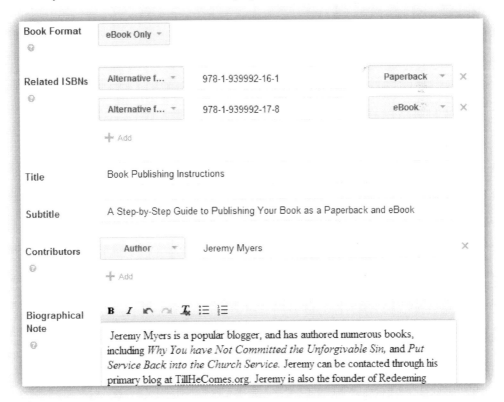

Once you have entered everything to your satisfaction, click the "Google Play settings" button the left to go to the next screen. The next screen is the prices and distribution settings. You can select individual prices for various currencies and countries, or just select your home-country currency and enter the price, and type in "world" for the distribution setting. The rest of the settings on this screen are unique to the way Google handles books. Note that you can allow people to copy/paste a percentage of your book if you want, and can say whether or not you want photos to appear in your eBook, and a few other items. If there is a question about any item, simply click the little gray question mark next to each option.

> *You can allow people to copy/paste a percentage of your book and can say whether or not you want photos to appear in your eBook.*

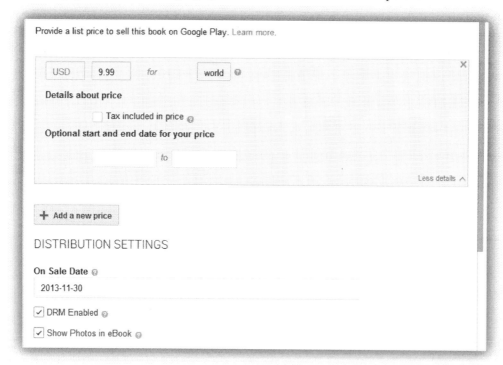

The next screen contains more settings for your Google Book. You can choose how much of your book people can preview online before they buy it (I recommend you stick with the default 20%), and Google also adds some options for how people can buy the book directly from your website or blog if you have it set up. You just need to have the page and links ready to go. At the time of writing this, I do not yet have these links, so I left them blank. I did, however, add my Publishing website and Publisher Logo.

The final screen is where you can upload your Content files. This is where you upload your book cover and manuscript files. Right now, Google only accepts PDF and ePub files for the interior of your book, so if you want to publish on Google Books and only have a Word document, you will need to go back and follow the steps outlined in the chapter on Formatting the eBook for publication and create the HTML file, which can then be used to create the ePub file for Google Books. Once you upload your files, click the "Save" button at the top, and Google will begin processing your files and checking them for errors.

Depending on the size of your files, this process of checking your content can take some time. My files for this book took about an hour to be approved. Once the files are approved, you can begin selling your book through Google Books.

❑ Publish Your eBook at Apple iBooks

I am not sure why, but for me, publishing an eBook at Apple for their iBooks store was the most challenging process of them all. It seemed that at every new step, there was something that had to be done which almost required me to start all over. So much for usability. (Being a PC person, I just had to make that jab.) The difficulties I experienced were numerous and varied, some of which I will try to explain as I go through the publishing process below.

Note, however, that if you want to sell your book on iBooks, but don't want the hassle of publishing directly on their platform, there are other ways. Later in this chapter, for example, I provide steps for publishing your eBook at Smashwords. Smashwords is an Apple iBook aggregator, which means that if you publish with Smashwords, they will list your book on the iBooks store for you.

But if you want to publish your eBook on Apple iBooks directly, it can be done using the guide below. There are few things to take note of, however, before you attempt to publish your eBook with Apple.

First, the primary method of publishing your eBook on Apple iBooks requires that your book file be in the ePub format (There is a second way of publishing your eBook which requires only the Microsoft Word document, but in my experience, this second method doesn't work very well). So if you chose not to convert your Word document to the HTML and then to the ePub format as outlined in the chapter on Formatting your eBook, you might want to go back and follow the steps in that chapter to create the HTML file, and then follow the steps which were listed earlier in this chapter for creating the ePub file. Alternately, Apple says that if you use their Pages program, it easily creates valid ePub files. I do not own Pages, so was not able to test it.

But once you have the ePub file, you still may not be able to sell your book on Apple iBooks. Why not? Apple requires that all booksellers have ISBN numbers from Bowker and an Employee Identification Number (EIN) from the IRS. If you have the ISBN, but have not registered with the IRS as a publishing company, you can still list your books with Apple, but you cannot sell them. You have to give them away for free. The only way to sell your books through Apple is to register with the IRS as a publishing company and obtain an EIN.

Even then, the Apple iBooks publishing software is only available to people who own a Mac computer, and who have the most recent version of the Apple Operating System, Apple OS 10.7.4 or later. The reason is that to publish on Apple, you need the Apple iTunes Producer program (and the optional iBooks Author application) which is only available on Mac computers.

So, to sum it all up: To publish and sell your book with Apple, you need:

- Validated ePub file
- ISBN from Bowker
- EIN from the IRS
- Mac computer running OS 10.7.4 or later

- Apple iTunes Producer
- (Optional) Apple iBooks Author

If you have all that, then you can publish with Apple. As you may have noticed through this book so far, I use a computer with Microsoft Windows and Microsoft Word. But thankfully, my wife has a Mac, and I recently upgraded it to OS X Mavericks. Also, since I have a publishing company registered with the IRS, and I have purchased ISBN numbers from Bowker, I have everything I need to publish with Apple.

If you do not have all these things, however, don't worry! You can still publish and sell your books with Apple. As I mentioned above, you can publish your eBook to Apple iBooks by publishing on Smashwords, which is the last publishing platform I discuss in this chapter. You don't need an ePub file, an ISBN number, an EIN number, or a Mac computer. All you need is your Microsoft Word document. Upload this document to their site, and they will do the rest. Nice, huh? The only drawback is that you lose some of your royalty payment to Smashwords. For most authors who do not have a publishing company or the technical know-how for submitting files to Apple, publishing through Smashwords is the only option available.

But if you are like me, and want more control over where all your books are sold, I provide the following guide for publishing your eBook directly with Apple. Below is the step-by-step guide for getting your book into the Apple iBooks store.

The first step is to log into the <u>iBooks</u> section of Apple iTunes Connect.

After you click the "Get Started" button, you will have to choose whether to give away your books or sell them. There are additional requirements for creating an account through which you can sell books. Choose the one which will help you accomplish your publishing goals. Obviously, if you are looking to sell your books, then this is the option you will need to choose, but only if you have the required elements mentioned above.

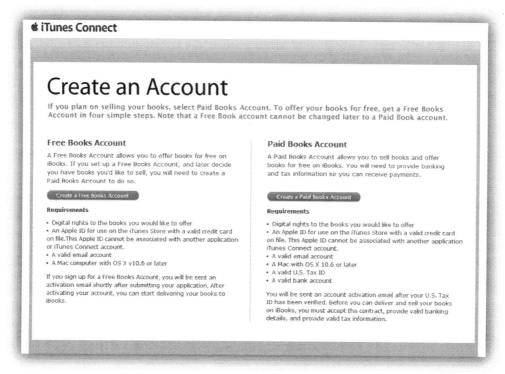

Once your account is set up, you can login at <u>iTunes Connect</u> to start creating your book. After you login you will need to agree to some legal contracts and update your banking information and other such details.

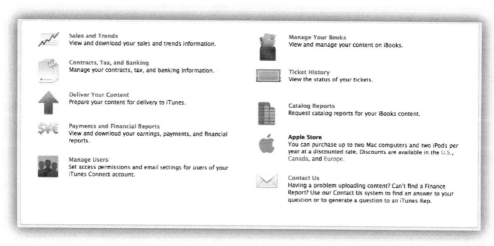

Once you have accepted and submitted all the required legal documents and banking details, you can begin the process of submitting your book. From the iTunes Connect screen, click the "Deliver Your Content" link. On this screen, you will see that there are two ways of delivering books to Apple iBooks. The first is with the iBooks Author application, and the second is with iTunes Producer. I will show you both, though no matter which route you choose, you will eventually end up publishing your book through iTunes Producer. The iBooks Author program was built to help authors navigate the difficulties of iTunes Producer, but after you create your book with iBooks Author, it exports the book to iTunes Producer before uploading it to the iBooks store.

To publish through iTunes Producer, you will need the validated ePub file which you created earlier in this chapter with the Calibre program. The nice thing about using the iBooks Author program, however, is that you can use your Microsoft Word document. However, even then, there are a few complications and difficulties to overcome.

For this guide, I will first show you how to create your book with iTunes Producer, and then I will provide a brief guide for publishing through iBooks Author.

To begin with, download, install, and launch the iTunes Producer program. It will ask you to accept some legal terms and login with your iTunes Connect account. Once you have logged in, you will be greeted with a screen which invites you to open or create a new package. Since you will be creating a new book, click the "Create New Package" button, and on the following screen, select "Book."

The first step to creating your new book with iTunes Producer should be quite familiar by now. It asks you for the ISBN number, the title, the book description, the publisher, and numerous other details about your book. Most of these can be gleaned from your Book Information Document which you created previously. Note that there are numerous screens on which to enter information about your book, including Categories, Authors, Target Audience, and Rights & Pricing. Make sure you enter as much information as possible.

After you enter all the Book information for your iBook, you go to the Assets screen. This is where you upload the validated ePub file you created earlier. You can also create a shortened version of your book for the preview file. This is the part of your book that people can preview for free. I am not going to create one of these for this guide. If you are having problems with your ePub

If you are having problems with your ePub not being accepted by iTunes Producer, you can also download the iBook Proofer from your iTunes Connect account.

not being accepted by iTunes Producer, you can also download the iBook Proofer from your iTunes Connect account. This program helps you create and validate your ePub files for use on iTunes Producer.

Also make sure you upload your eBook cover art and any other interior screenshots which you might things are helpful for your book.

Apple iTunes Producer makes sure you have added all the necessary details for your book, and checks to make sure your ePub file validates correctly.

The final step is to make sure that all your files are valid and accepted. When you click the "Next" button, Apple iTunes Producer makes sure you have added all the necessary details for your book, and checks to make sure your ePub file validates correctly. Hopefully, this is the screen you see:

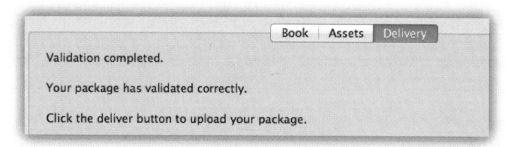

If you files are valid and you have entered all the necessary details, click "Deliver" and all the files will upload to Apple iBooks for publication. They will go through a process much like every other publishing site you have submitted your book to, and if anything else is needed, or if there are further errors, you will be notified by email. If your book is accepted for publication, you will receive an email notification about that as well.

So that is how to publish your eBook on the Apple iBooks store using iTunes Producer. Apple has recently released the Apple iBooks Author program, which is another way to publish your book on the iBooks store. In my experience, while this program initially seems easier (because you can upload your Word document), it ends up not being easier. The iBooks Author program does not properly read your imported styles and settings from your Word document, and it takes hours and hours of tweaking to get the book to work and appear properly in this program. Note that even if you use iBooks Author, you will still end up submitting your files to iTunes Producer before delivery to iBooks, so make sure you are somewhat familiar with the steps listed above.

To use iBooks Author, first download it from the App Store, and then launch the program. You will be greeted with the following screen:

Choose whichever format you prefer, but for most books which have the traditional look and feel, the Landscape with Portrait "Basic" style is probably the best. Once you click on it, you will be greeted with the book template screen. Before you start importing text, you should look over the template pages to make sure you like what you see. If you want to change anything on the template, you can do so by going to the "View" button and selecting "Show Layouts." The Layout options appear in the sidebar, and from here you can change the look and feel of the book template. You can change the chapter titles, page headings, fonts, and even page background color. For this book, I am going to change nothing.

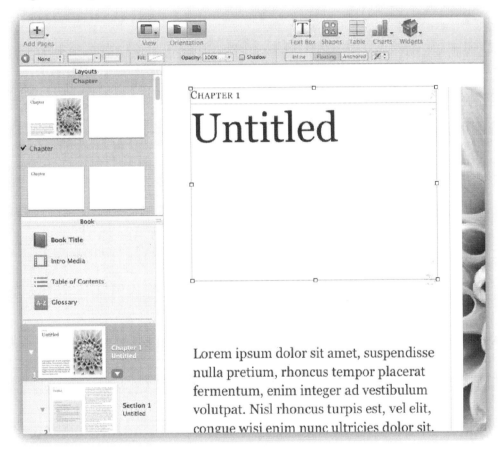

Once you have edited your layout options, the next thing we are going to do is change the Book Cover. In Apple iBooks Author, this is the "Book Title" page. Click on it, and you will see the current default layout for your eBook cover. All you need to do is delete all the elements that are already on the Book Title page, and then insert the premade eBook cover onto this screen. You can do this by finding the eBook cover on your computer, and then dragging and dropping it onto the page. Some resizing might be required to get it to fit.

The next thing to do is insert the text of your book. Apple iBooks Author actually makes this quite simple. All you need to do is drag and drop your Microsoft Word document into the Book Text area of your Screen. The program will process the Book and insert it. The program will ask you which layout you want to use for the import. You may want to try a few of the options here, but for my book, since I already have chapter titles and interior images, I did not want that first page of each chapter to have a sort of "Cover page" which the Title, a summary, and an image. So I chose to import the book as "Section Text." This layout seemed closest to what I actually had in my Word document.

Note that there will likely be some trial and error for how your book needs to be imported properly, and there will likely be

Note that there will likely be some trial and error for how your book needs to be imported properly, and there will likely be a few warnings or errors about things that were changed during the import process.

a few warnings or errors about things that were changed during the import process, but once you get it close to the way you want the book to look, you should go back through the book, page by page, and make any corrections to chapter titles or image placement that needs to be made. Also, you can change your chapter and section titles in the Book Outline menu on the left.

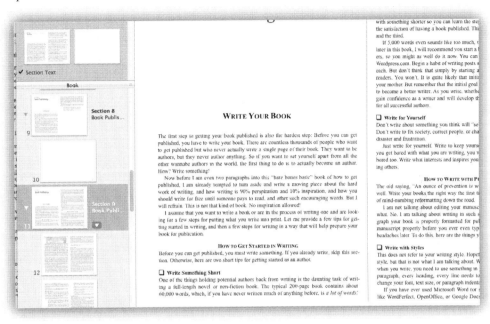

If you properly prepared the Word document using styles as explained in this book, Apple iBooks Author will do a pretty good job of importing the book in a way that looks clean and professional. Note, however, that importing your book as a "Section" will mess up the iBooks Table of Contents. Specifically, there will not be any actual Table of Contents. Ideally, iBooks Author wants each chapter and each section of the book to be imported separately, which requires you to import the Title page all by itself, then Chapter 1 with each subsection, then Chapter 2 with its subsections, and so on. To do this, you would need to open your Word document and cut it up into numerous files, one for each chapter and section. This way, the iBook Table of Contents will be properly populated with the various chapter and section headings, which will create the best overall appearance for your book.

If you properly prepared the Word document using styles as explained in this book, Apple iBooks Author will do a pretty good job of importing the book in a way that looks clean and professional.

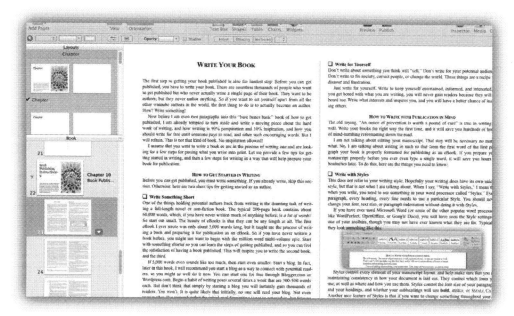

When your book is finished, make sure you preview it in iBooks.

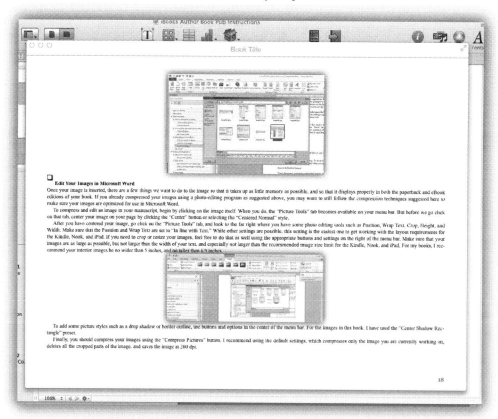

If the book looks good, click the "Publish" button. You will now enter a process which should be pretty familiar by now. After you sign into to your iTunes

Connect account which was created earlier, and you are given the choice of which section of your book to offer as a preview of the book, and as a last step, iBooks Author tells you that it will export the book over to iTunes Producer to finish the setup and publishing process.

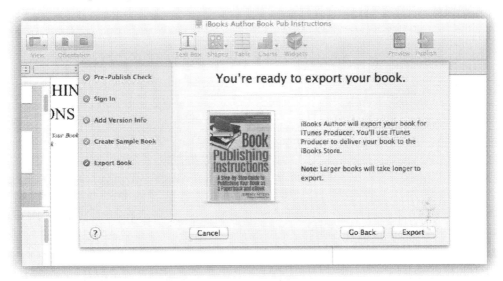

At this point, the publishing process picks up with publishing through iTunes Producer which was covered above.

This completes the guide for publishing your eBook on the iBooks store. Apple is making lots of changes to their publishing platform in order to keep up with the ever-changing eBook publishing world, and I expect that in the near future, the process of publishing with Apple will get even easier.

Let us move on, however, to a publishing platform that is one of the leading eBook companies in the world, and which will also send your eBook over to the Apple iBooks store for you if you desire.

❑ Publish Your eBook at Smashwords

No matter which eBook publishing sources you choose from the options above, I highly recommend that you also publish your book at <u>Smashwords</u>. They are one of the industry leaders in eBook publishing, and in many ways are revolutionizing the publishing world. Truly, Smashwords provides one-stop-shopping for all forms of eBooks. Through Smashwords, you can publish your book as a PDF for people who want to read it on their computer, as a Mobi for the Kindle, and as an ePub for the iPad, Nook, and other digital eReaders. Smashwords also publishes the book as an HTML file. Like the Amazon KDP Select program, you can choose to give away your eBook for free, but Smashwords also provides the option of offering sales, coupons, and special offers.

Most beautiful of all, Smashwords doesn't have that exclusivity requirement which Amazon does. Smashwords does not require that you list your book *only* with them in order to take advantage of all that Smashwords offers. Also, as indicated in the previous section, Smashwords has an agreement with Apple to sell your book on the Apple iBooks store. Smashwords serves as your publisher, and they provide you with the required ISBN so that you can list your book. Publishing at Smashwords is really a win-win for everybody involved, and I wish Smashwords great success as the publishing world continues to evolve. Some may think that nobody can complete with Amazon, but in many ways, I believe that Amazon is trying to "catch-up" to Smashwords.

Now, having said all this, due to the ability of Smashwords to get your book onto the Apple iBooks store, and so that your files can be published in all of the popular eBook formats, Smashwords has some minor additional formatting requirements that have not yet been explained in this book. However, if you followed the paperback and eBook formatting guidelines in the earlier chapters of this book, the necessary changes are quite minor. Smashwords has their own "Formatting Guidelines" document, and most of what has been written in this book was written with the Smashwords guidelines in mind. In fact, the very first eBook I ever wrote (*The Lie*) was written with nothing but the Smashwords Publishing Guide, and every subsequent eBook that I have published has tried to remain within their publishing guidelines so that my eBooks could easily get published on their platform. So even though you have my guide in front of you, I also recommend you download and read the free *Smashwords Style Guide* by Mark Coker.

Ultimately, if you have followed the steps in this guide up to this point, there is only one change that needs to be made to your manuscript for acceptance into the Smashwords platform. All you need to do is edit your copyright page to indicate that this is the Smashwords edition.

To do this simple change, it is critical that you are working with the proper document. If you remember back when you created several different versions of your Word document for various uses, one of the Word documents you created was for the eBook publishing platforms. After making some edits to that Word document, you saved it as an actual HTML file. To make the edit necessary for Smashwords, you want to open that Word document from which you made the HTML file. You *do not* want to open the HTML file itself. If you followed the guide in this book, this file will be a Word document with "eBook" as part of the file name. So go back and find that Word document which was specially created for your eBook files. Open it with Microsoft Word.

The first thing you are going to do is save it as your "Smashwords" Word document. You should already have three Word documents in there, one for the paperback edition, one for the eBook edition, and one as a backup. You now want to create a new file specifically for Smashwords. However, if you are using any version of Microsoft Word after Word 2003, you cannot simply save the document as it is. For some reason, Smashwords requires that the Word document have the older ".doc" file extension from Microsoft Word 97-2003 rather than the newer ".docx" extension. So if you have a newer version of Microsoft Word, when you save your file, make sure you choose "Word 97-2003" from the drop-down menu on the Save As screen.

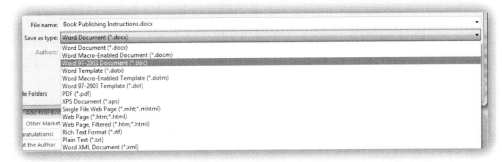

Now that you have the Word document you are going to edit for Smashwords, you are ready to make the one required edit to the file. Scroll down to the copyright page, and find the part near the top where the copyright is actually listed. On my page, it says "© 2013 by Jeremy Myers." Right underneath this line, include the words "Smashwords Edition." To publish on the Smashwords platform, Smashwords requires that you have this on the copyright page. They have some other recommendations for this page as well, but this is the only required change. You can see their other recommendations by accessing the *Smashwords Style Guide*.

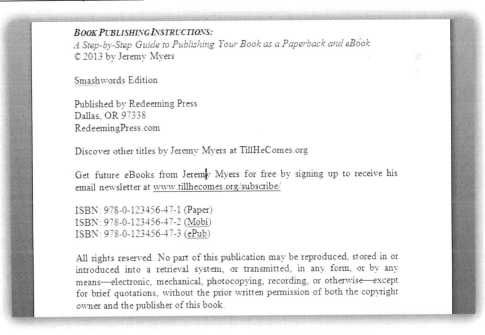

Save your file, remembering to check that it is still in the Word 97-2003 file format, and then head on over to Smashwords to publish your eBook.

To publish with Smashwords, login to your Smashwords account, and click the "Publish" button near the top. A screen will open in which you enter all the details about your book just as you have done many times previously on other platforms. Once again, remember that you cannot do this if you have enrolled your book in Amazon's KDP Select program. Enter the book title, book description, price, and book category, all of which you can pull from your Book Information Document. Upload your eBook cover and the Smashwords Word document you just created, and then let the Smashwords meatgrinder and AutoVetter do their thing.

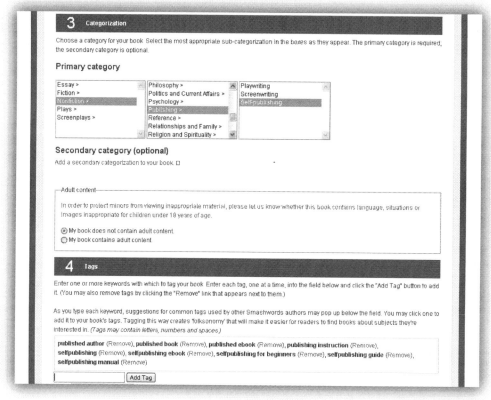

Note that you may have to go through several rounds of uploading your document and correcting any errors that are found by the AutoVetter program. For example, with this current book, the file size was too large due to all of my embedded images, so I had to compress all the images down to a "Web/Screen" resolution of 96 dpi to get the Word document under the maximum allowable file size of 10 MB.

If your book uploads properly and you receive no errors, you can go to your Smashwords Dashboard to check on the progress of your book.

If you ever need to change anything in your book, you will also do it from this screen. Once it is published, the red section on the right will turn to green if everything has been formatted properly, and the book will now be ready for sale. If there are warning in that red section, you should try to fix whatever errors it provides. Also, if you ever want to unpublish your book, you can do so by clicking the "unpublish" link in the Status column. Once your book is published on the Smashwords platform, you can begin to promote it, create coupons, increase the affiliate percentage, or whatever else you want to do to help people buy and read your book.

You have now published your book as a paperback and an eBook in numerous formats and on various websites. Congratulations! Not only are you a published author, but as people begin to find your book on various sites, it lends more credibility to your status as an author, and more people are likely to buy your book.

However, the work of being a published author is not done. Not only do you need to start writing your next book, but the even harder work of marketing and selling your book has only just begun. This is the topic in the final chapter.

MARKETING YOUR BOOK

Even though you publish a book, there is no guarantee of sales. In fact, most self-published authors sell less than 100 copies. This is one reason that new and aspiring authors seek to get published through a traditional publishing company. They think that publishing companies will help them with marketing and selling their book. While most publishing companies will help the author do a tiny bit of marketing, the reality is that the vast majority of publishing companies expect the author to do most of the marketing and publicity of their book.

One of the dirty little secrets of the publishing world is that publishers don't care about the content of your book as much as they care about whether or not you will be able to market and sell your book. It is not an exaggeration to say that the number one factor a publishing company considers when trying to decide which books to print is whether or not the author has the ability to sell books. While we would like to think that publishing companies pick books to print based on the ideas they contain and the style of writing, the honest truth is that these are only secondary considerations. The main thing publishing companies want to see is marketability, that is, how well can the author generate buzz about his or her book, and how many copies can he or she sell through their author platform. Getting publishing is not going to help you find readers; you need to have lots of readers (or the ability to gain them) *before* you get published.

This is one reason that self-publishing is a good route for new and aspiring authors. It not only helps new authors get into print when traditional publishing companies will probably not even consider their book, but it also helps authors begin to develop their writing platform and grow a following. Once this happens, it is quite likely that several traditional publishing companies will take notice, and will reach out to you for your next book, rather than you having to send query letters to them.

So one of the things you need to do in the process of publishing your book is get accustomed to the fact that getting your book into print is only the first step in becoming an author. Once your book is available, the next step is getting your book read. Though there is huge satisfaction to seeing your book in print, there is even greater satisfaction to seeing your book in people's hands. For this to happen, you will have to do some marketing and promoting of your book.

When it comes to marketing your book, there really is no limit to what you can do. This chapter will provide some suggestions and ideas to get you started.

❑ Blog About Your Book

It sometimes shocks me how many aspiring authors I meet who do not have blogs. While I do not claim to know the heart and mind and technical know-how of most authors, I wonder how much a writer really wants to write if they don't do much writing. Yes, I suppose some writers might just write on their computer or in notebooks, but if you are a writer that wants to be read, why would you not put your writing in a place where people can read it?

There is no better way of finding a reading audience than through a blog.

If a local newspaper came to you and said, "We want you to write a weekly column but we cannot pay you," would you do it? You probably would jump at the opportunity! Well, this is what blogging is, except that rather than write for a local newspaper, you are writing for a worldwide newspaper. Sure, there are millions of other people writing as well, but there are also billions of readers!

I firmly believe that all writers should have a blog. Blogs are essential for today's authors.

Aside from the benefit of finding readers, blogging also helps you practice your writing skills. Blogging helps you find your voice and teaches you to write concisely and with consistency. All writers become better writers through blogging.

Once you have written a book, a blog is also a great way to tell others about your book, help people learn what your book is about, and allow your reading audience to connect with you, the author. Gone are the days when people go into a bookstore and decide whether or not to read a book by looking at the back cover. Today, people look up the book online, learn about the author through his or her blog, read online book reviews, and check out a sample chapter or two if they are available. All of these can be put on your blog.

If you are unsure about how to start a blog or how to write one, don't be concerned. If you can type a book in Microsoft Word, you can write a blog. Some platforms are free, but I highly recommend a self-hosted blog, as they are more professional looking and have many more options that will help the serious-minded author. If you are concerned about cost, a self-hosted blog will only run about $5 a month. I will even help you get it <u>set up for free</u>. For those authors who are looking to get published through Redeeming Press, we <u>offer our authors an incredible deal on a new blog</u>. We provide fast and reliable Wordpress hosting, and use of the best premium blog theme on the market: the <u>Genesis Framework by StudioPress</u>.

If you start a blog, make sure you enable comments on your blog posts. I am always shocked to find that some authors have the comments on their blog turned off. I understand that allowing comments gives people the freedom to say snarky things on your blog, challenge your ideas, or even to leave inane remarks, but turning comments off is somewhat like telling your readers that you don't care what they have to say; all you want is to talk to them, but not let them talk to you.

And when people leave comments, reply to them! Again, I am always shocked to look at the blogs of some authors, and they never reply to the comments that people leave on their blog posts. I understand that if you are getting dozens of comments on each post you may not have the time to respond to all of them, but even popular bloggers should respond to some of the comments. It is a way to tell your readers that you care about them, value them, and are interested in what they say. For most of my blogging history, I have tried to respond to every single comment that people leave. In recent years, this is getting impossible as people leave more comments, but interacting with my readers will always be a high priority.

Even if you are months or years away from publishing a book, don't wait to get published before you start your blog. The best time to start a blog is today. If, on the other hand, you are an established author and are trying to reach out to new readers, don't spend tons of money on marketing campaigns and expensive advertisements. You too should start a blog today.

❑ Start an Email Newsletter

Along with a blog, you should also start an email newsletter. Though blogs are great to help you find readers, email newsletters are the best way to stay in touch with readers who want a more intimate connection with one of their favorite authors. Getting blog readers is good, but getting email newsletter subscribers is even better, because such readers are giving you permission to send them an email into their inbox. This means that they value what you write, and want to stay in touch.

Email newsletter recipients are some of the valuable connections you will make in your marketing efforts. These are people who appreciate what you have written before, and want to be updated about new releases, any book tour or speaking opportunities that might allow them to meet you, and any other pertinent news which you think they might want to hear.

Ultimately, the email newsletter provides the personal touch to your reading audience that is not often possible through a book by itself.

Of course, along with this, you must treat your subscribers like friends. The email newsletter should be free, and you must promise to never send spam, to never sell their email address, and to always allow them to unsubscribe at any time for any reason whatsoever. A person's email address is a valuable piece of information, and you must treat it as such.

And just like a blog, the best time to start an email newsletter is today. If you have a blog, you can put a sign-in form on your website. If you speak at conferences, do radio interviews, or go on book tours, make sure you invite people to sign up whenever and wherever you can. One thing I have found in growing my own email newsletter list is that it helps to provide an incentive to people for signing up, such as a free eBook or some sort of special report or insider's news.

There are numerous sites which will help you set up an email list and start collecting people's email addresses and sending out the email for you. There are three that I recommend. One of them is free, and the other two cost a bit of money. Of course, even the free newsletter site will eventually start charging you if your mailing list grows to more than 2000 people.

My pattern was this: I started with the free email newsletter provider, which is <u>Mailchimp</u>, and then once my list grew to 2000 people, I moved over to <u>AWeber</u>, as I think they provide more of the services and options I desired. I have also heard people recommend <u>Constant Contact</u>, but I have never used them. They tend to be a bit cheaper than AWeber, but overall, <u>AWeber</u> tends to get better reviews online.

My practice regarding my email newsletter is to give away a free eBook to all newsletter subscribers immediately upon subscribing. Then, every time I complete a new eBook, I give this new book away as well to all current subscribers. Though I have never heard of someone else doing this, I believe in the power of "free" and this is one more way I say "Thanks" to those who subscribe to my email newsletter. This practice might also keep them from unsubscribing. This book you hold in your hands was initially given away for free to newsletter subscribers.

Those who subscribe have the option to get daily updates of my blog posts, or receive a weekly digest, which includes summaries of all the posts I wrote this week. Some choose to receive both, which is pretty cool. Then, about once a month or so, I send out an "Insider's News" email, which includes blog information, personal updates, special news, and insider announcements which is not available to anyone else. Only those who subscribe to the email newsletter get these special monthly reports. Sometimes they include invitations to participate in a book project, or provide offers on other free books I know about.

One final benefit to using an email list is that you can also sell your books to email subscribers. People who subscribe to your email list typically want to know about you and your books. So you can offer special sales or two-for-one deals to your email subscribers on books they might not yet have. I even use auto-responder emails to help inform new email subscribers about my others books, and give them limited-time offers on getting my previous books at steeply discounted prices. Along with AWeber's auto-responder email, I use a program called <u>Scarcity Samurai</u> to help me send out these emails (the free version of <u>Mailchimp</u> does not allow auto-responder emails, which is another reason to use <u>AWeber</u>). <u>Scarcity Samurai</u> can also be used to help boost book sales through your email newsletter and book launch campaign.

❑ **Get Social**

One key to letting others know about your book is to develop relationships and friendships with them. But how are you going to do this with people on the other side of the country or around the world? Thanks to the internet, this is becoming easier every day. To connect with potential readers, it is essential for authors to create personal accounts on social websites such as Facebook, Twitter, Google+, Pinterest, and YouTube. You don't necessarily have to be on all of these sites, but I strongly recommend at least the first two: Facebook and Twitter.

Note, however, that spreading the word about your book on these sites is not done by sending Facebook updates and Tweets about your book all the time. You must view social sites as if you were having an actual conversation with someone, with the only difference being that they are not standing right in front of you. True conversations are never one sided and are never on only one topic. In any conversation, there is genuine give and take. There is interest in the other person, in what they are saying, in what they think. There are questions and discussions about a wide variety of topics and issues. This is also how you should converse with people on social sites. Don't just write about yourself. Interact with other people. Get interested in their posts, and what they have to say. Ask questions. Respond. Reply. Share posts and ideas from other people. Be social!

After you start a Facebook and Twitter account, I recommend you slowly expand into some of the other social platforms, such as Google+, Pinterest, and YouTube. Google+ is a lot like Facebook, so once you are familiar with Facebook, learning to use Google+ will be a breeze. Pinterest is a picture-sharing site, so you will want to include interesting and compelling images on your blog which you can share on Pinterest. If you use YouTube, you will want to create helpful or informative videos which you can post on YouTube and on your blog. Somewhere along the way, you may want to create a Podcast as well, and put it on Apple iTunes.

As a side note, if you have a blog, one plugin I highly recommend is called Social Network Auto Poster. This plugin will add your blog posts to all your social networks. When you publish a blog post, it will send out a Tweet about it, add a notice to Facebook, put it on Google+, add a page to StumbleUpon, publish an image from your post to Pinterest, and so on. This plugin is a great way to let all your social network followers receive updates that a new blog post has been published.

By the way, if you want to interact with me on any of these social sites, here are some of the sites you can connect with me on the internet. I hope to see you online!

- Facebook Page
- Facebook Profile
- Twitter
- Google+

- LinkedIn
- YouTube
- Pinterest
- Podcast

Another great way of being social is by reading the blogs of other people and commenting on their posts. Reading and commenting on other people's blogs will not only give you tips and ideas on what to write about on your blog, but will also help the readers (and authors) of other blogs find your blog. Very early in the history of my blog, I tried to leave 5-10 comments a day on other blogs around the internet. I am convinced that this was one reason my blog traffic saw slow but steady growth over the first few years of my blog's existence.

If you find a really good blog post, feel free to quote a paragraph from it on your own blog, and link back to it from your own blog, or share it on Facebook, Twitter, and Google+. This is not only a good social practice, but when people see that you are sharing their content, they are more likely to share and recommend your content.

Ultimately, the golden rule also applies to blogging and social sites: Do unto others as you would have them do unto you. You want people to read your blog? Read theirs. You want people to leave comments on your site? Leave comments on theirs. You want people to share your content? Share theirs.

❑ Use Amazon's KDP Select

Amazon offers a program to their eBook authors called KDP Select. This program offers special incentives and rewards to Amazon authors, but there are some restrictions as well. Essentially, if you put your book in the KDP Select program, you are not allowed to publish your book on any other platform or website for a minimum of 90 days. During this 90-day period, however, customers who are Amazon Prime members can read your book without paying for it, and at the end of the month, Amazon pays you a certain amount of money based on how many times your book was read. The amount changes every month, and the amount you receive depends on how many people read your book, so it is impossible to say how much money you might get by participating in KDP Select.

But this is not the real reason I enroll my books in KDP Select. The reason you should join KDP Select is because during the 90-day enrollment period, you can offer your eBook as a free download for up to five days. Since I always give all my eBooks away for free when they are first published, I love making use of Amazon's customer base to give away my eBooks. Doing so not only helps people learn about me as an author, but also provides long-term benefits to the ranking of my book in the Amazon best-sellers lists. While I do not know exactly how Amazon calculates their best-seller lists, I have noticed that all the books I have given away for free through the KDP Select program consistently rank higher than the books which I have not enrolled in the KDP Select program. This is because one of the ranking factors on Amazon is "Total books sold" and since thousands of people download my eBooks when they are offered for free on Amazon, this causes the long-term ranking of these books to be much higher than they would be otherwise.

Technically, if you stayed in enrolled in the Amazon KDP Select program, you could offer your eBook on Amazon as a free download for five days every three months. The problem with this, however, is that once you set up this pattern, you will probably generate very few sales. Readers will soon realize that if they want one of your books, all they have to do is wait a few months to get it for free. Maybe this is what you want to do, as this could really help build your audience platform. But this is probably not the best approach to use if you want to make some income from your book sales.

My approach is as follows. First, I upload the book to Kindle Direct Publishing, enroll the book in KDP Select, and schedule the five-day free giveaway. I then announce on my blogs and through my free email newsletter that the book will be available for free. During those days, thousands of people go and download the book, and as a result, I often make several top-ten Amazon best-selling lists in the "Free" section of various Amazon categories. I do not make any money off these downloads, but I do connecting with readers around the world who may not have read one of my books in any other way.

If you don't want to give your books away for free, you could use another service offered through KDP Select called "Kindle Countdown" to start selling your eBook. This service allows you to start the price of the book at several dollars lower than the normal list price, and then every day the price goes up by a certain amount, until it reaches the full list price of the book. Such a feature taps into the psychological desire of humans to not miss out on a sale. So, for example, if your book is selling for $7.99, the first day of the Kindle Countdown offer could be $2.99. Then after 24 hours, it will increase to $3.99, and so forth, until after five days, it reaches the normal list price for the eBook. Managing the promotion this way allows you to begin to ramp up sales of the book following its release.

Whichever promotion you choose, after it is finished, you can cancel the KDP Select enrollment for that book so that it will not renew at the end of the 90-day period. Then, while you wait for the 90 days to expire, you can prepare to publish your book on Barnes & Noble, Google Books, Apple iBooks, Smashwords, and any other websites. You can also use this time to prepare the necessary blog posts and email announcements for when the book goes live on those sites. Once the 90 days conclude for the KDP Select program, simply hit the "Publish" buttons (or their equivalent) wherever else you are publishing the eBook, and announce on your blog and email newsletter that the book is now available elsewhere.

This may not be a pattern you want to follow, but based on my publishing goals and how I like to give away my eBooks for free, this is a system that has worked quite well for me over the past several years.

If you want to publish your eBook right away on as many platforms as possible and so cannot use KDP Select, then I highly recommend that you at least offer some sort of "New Release" sale for the first 3-5 days the book is available. Offer it initially for $0.99 (or something else rather low) and then after the promotion period is over, raise the price to the regular price for your book. Again, the goal is to generate as much buys and buzz as possible during the initial release of the book. As your book rises in Amazon's best seller's lists, you will likely gain some new readers. Once a reader likes one of your books, they are likely to buy your others as well.

Sign up your eBook for the Amazon Matchbook program.

One other form of book marketing that works well through Amazon is to sign up your eBook for the Amazon Matchbook program. This only applies if you are also printing your book as a paperback on Amazon CreateSpace. This promotional offer allows people who buy the paperback book on Amazon to also get the eBook at a discounted rate. If your paperback book is $9.99, and the normal price for your eBook is $7.99, people will typically only purchase one or the other. But the Matchbook program encourages people to buy both. If they purchase the paperback book at $9.99, they will be given the opportunity to also purchase the eBook at a discounted rate which you set, say for $1.99. With the rise in popularity of eBooks, this is a great way to allow people to get both the paperback and the eBook versions of your books at a reasonable rate.

Amazon is your best friend as a self-publisher. Make sure you understand their policies and pricing structure, as they are interested in helping you sell as many books as possible and reaching as many readers as possible. Due to the worldwide popularity of Amazon, and how Kindle eBooks can be read on the iPad and other digital eReaders, Amazon may be the only site on which you publish your books. In fact, there are a couple other resources which Amazon provides to authors which we turn to next.

❑ Create an Author Page at Amazon

If you are publishing your books on Amazon, one thing you should consider doing is creating an Author Page. If you search for a book on Amazon, you will notice that one the book details page, you can often click the name of the author to see more about him or her. These author pages can have the image of the author, a biography, links to their blogs and social sites, as well as other books published by this author.

Here, for example, is my author page:

I really should probably add more text to my author biography section, but you notice that beneath the image and biography section it shows a list of my books, and recent Tweets and blog posts appear over on the right. This is just one more way for potential readers on Amazon to learn more about you as an author, and find you on the web.

To create an author page at Amazon, simply go to the <u>Author Central section of Amazon</u>, create an account, and add as many details as you want. You can always return and edit more details later. Once you have created an account, you can check your sales numbers, book rank, author rank, and a whole host of other items related to your books.

Every time you publish a book on Amazon, make sure you link it with your Author Central web page. Amazon will not do this automatically, but it can easily be done within the "Books" tab of your Author Central page. Just click "Add More Books," and then find your book on Amazon and add it to your profile. It is that easy. As you publish more books and as people leave reviews, make sure you return to your Author Central page to update the information and leave more details about your books.

❑ **Add Your Book to Goodreads**
When I first started using Goodreads, it was an independent site on which authors could post their books and interact with other readers and authors about their books. Since that time, Goodreads has been acquired by Amazon, and so I am not certain what the future holds for this site. Will Amazon incorporate it somehow into their Author Central Page? Will the data you enter at Author Central automatically update and populate your information over at Goodreads? I do not know.

But until more is learned about how Amazon is going to incorporate Goodreads into their ever-expanding publishing empire, you can continue to use Goodreads the same way that you use Author Central at Amazon. You can create an account on their site, add your book titles, enter an author biography, and include all the same details as you did on Amazon's Author Central. Again, the reason for doing this is that the more places you have your books listed, the more likely it is that people will find your book and connect with you as a published author. If this is something you want to do, you will first have to create an author profile at Goodreads.com. Do this by reading their author guide and signing up to participate in the Goodreads author program. Once you are in, you will be given access to an author dashboard which can be set up with information similar to what you posted on Amazon.

Once you login at Goodreads, you can add your book through your Dashboard. If the book is already listed, then this means that Amazon has begun to populate the Goodreads pages with the details that have been entered at Amazon Author Central. But until that begins to happen (which has not happened at the time of writing this), you can manually enter the book yourself onto the Goodreads website. To do this, go to the Add New Book page, and search for you title, just as you did with Amazon. If it does not find your book, you can click the "Manually add a book" link which is to the right of the search box, and enter all the pertinent information that it asks for. Don't forget to add a book cover using the "Add Book Cover" link. You should follow these steps for both the paperback and eBook versions of your book.

Once you have added the paperback and eBook editions of your book to Goodreads, you should combine them so that when people search for them online, both editions are shown together. Combining your editions can be done through your personal author page on Goodreads. From the Author Dashboard, click on "My Books" and there should be a "Combine Editions" link in the upper right-hand corner.

Below is a screenshot of my author dashboard at Goodreads.

There is a lot more you can do at Goodreads, such as upload a PDF or ePub version of your book to sell on Goodreads, start an author blog, interact with other readers and authors, post reviews, keep track of reading lists and wanted books, and a variety of other similar items. Goodreads somewhat functions as a Facebook for book authors and book readers, and it can be a great tool to connect with other authors, find readers, and promote your own book.

❏ Hold a Book Launch Party

One proven strategy for generating interest and sales in your book is to host a book launch party. I have not yet personally done this myself, but plan to do so in the future (If you want to participate, make sure you subscribe to my Redeeming Press email newsletter to receive updates and offers). A book launch can work with either paperback books or eBooks.

First, gather together 50 to 100 bloggers who have a decent amount of readers and who will agree to read a pre-release copy of your book and then review it on their own blog and on Amazon.com during the release week. Send them a free copy of the book about a month before the release date of the book, and tell them that they should read it and prepare a blog post about the book and a review of the book, both of which should be published during the book release week.

Second, it might be a good idea to offer a package of free extras for anyone who buys the book during that week. For example, people who buy the book that week could be given a free copy of one of your other eBooks, a special training course, or some sort of personal guide or gift that will help or benefit the reader in some tangible way. Be creative and be generous. These bonus offers should also be mentioned by the bloggers who read and review your book.

When the launch week arrives, be as active as possible on Facebook, Twitter, and the blogs of all those who read and reviewed your book. Remember, the goal is not really to sell books, but to make connections with people, build relationships, and help people get to know you as the author. If you can do that, not only will you sell books, but you will build an audience for future books as well.

❑ **Other Marketing Ideas**

This chapter could go on with more ideas and examples of how to promote your book. For example, authors should make a habit of sending out free review copies to other bloggers. Ask them to read it and write a review on their blog and on Amazon.com. Or you could send your book to popular podcasters and radio show hosts to see if they would be interested in interviewing you. Some authors like to host readings down at the local bookstore or public library, but in my opinion, these sorts of events are relics of the old (and dying) publishing world. Mark Coker, the founder and creator of Smashwords, has published two books on marketing your eBook, both of which I highly recommend. They are the *Smashwords Book Marketing Guide* and *The Secrets to eBook Publishing Success*. They are free, so go download them both!

The bottom line is that when it comes to marketing your book, there is no failed attempt. Even if you try something and don't sell any books, you still raised awareness of your book in the minds of some people, and maybe they will buy your next book.

Let me close this chapter by encouraging you to see book marketing as one crucial element to book authoring. Though most authors do not like the marketing side of writing, book marketing is something that authors must embrace if they are going to be successful. Nobody is going to care about your book as much as you do. If you don't care about letting people know you've written a book, nobody else is going to care either. If you have written a book, you've got to market your book. While getting your book into print is a huge success, it is an even greater success to get your book into people's hands, and for that, you need to do some marketing.

To get you started in marketing, read the last chapter of this book to learn about one person who would love to read about your publishing success!

CONGRATULATIONS!

I hope this guide to publishing your book has been helpful and instructive. But most of all, I hope it has been encouraging. If you are like most authors, you have world-changing ideas dancing around in your head, and you have dreamt of getting these ideas onto paper and into print, but aside from telling your spouse about your book idea, or maybe starting a blog, you really haven't done much to help your book see the light of day.

Hopefully, this book changes that. Hopefully, this book gives you the step-by-step instructions you need to not only write your book, but also to get it printed so that people can read your book.

In fact, if this book helped you get your book into print, I want to read it! If you want to send me a copy of your book, I would love to read it, and maybe even write about it on one of my blogs or recommend your book on Amazon. To take advantage of this offer, send a copy of your book to the following address:

Jeremy Myers
Book Review Offer
PO Box 284
Sheridan, OR 97378

It has been my privilege and honor to help you get your book into print, and would love to see the fruit of your hard work and effort. When you do get published, I want to be one of the first people to say: "Congratulations on becoming a published author!"

ABOUT THE AUTHOR

Jeremy Myers is an author of numerous books and writes at TillHeComes.org, a popular blog about following Jesus into the world. His greatest accomplishment in life, however, is raising three beautiful daughters with his wife, Wendy.

Jeremy is also the founder and owner of Redeeming Press, a publishing company built upon the idea that books should be published based on the ideas they contain, rather than on how many copies they will sell. If you are an author who has been rejected by traditional publishing houses because you are not a popular conference speaker, mega church pastor, or radio personality, consider submitting your book to Redeeming Press for publication. Even if you haven't tried to publish through other companies, we would be thrilled to talk with you about publishing your book.

If you appreciated the content of the book and want to get a free quick-start publishing guide based on the content you have read in the preceding pages, you may sign up to receive the free Redeeming Press newsletter. And hey, if you really appreciated the book, how about recommending it to your friends or leaving a 5-Star Review on Amazon? Thanks!

CONNECT WITH JEREMY MYERS

If you want to read some of my other writings or connect with me through Twitter, Facebook, or one of my other social sites, here are some sites where you can do so. I look forward to meeting you online!

TillHeComes.org
RedeemingPress.com
GraceCommentary.com
Twitter.com/jeremyers1
Facebook.com/jeremy.myers3
Google.com/+JeremyMyers
Pinterest.com/jeremyers1
LinkedIn
iTunes Podcast

Put Service Back Into the Church Service

Churches around the world are trying to revitalize their church services. There is almost nothing they will not try. Some embark on multi-million dollar building campaigns while others sell their buildings to plant home churches. Some hire celebrity pastors to attract crowds of people, while others hire no clergy so that there can be open sharing in the service.

Yet despite everything churches have tried, few focus much time, money, or energy on the one thing that churches are supposed to be doing: loving and serving others like Jesus.

Put Service Back into the Church Service challenges readers to follow a few simple principles and put a few ideas into practice which will help churches of all types and sizes make serving others the primary emphasis of a church service.

Reviews from Amazon

Jeremy challenges church addicts, those addicted to an unending parade of church buildings, church services, Bible studies, church programs and more to follow Jesus into our communities, communities filled with lonely, hurting people and BE the church, loving the people in our world with the love of Jesus. Do we need another training program, another seminar, another church building, a remodeled church building, more staff, updated music, or does our world need us, the followers of Jesus, to BE the church in the world? The book is well-written, challenging and a book that really can make a difference not only in our churches, but also and especially in our neighborhoods and communities. –Charles Epworth

Do you ever have an unexplained frustration with your church, its service or programs? Do you ever feel like you are "spinning your wheels" when it comes to reaching others for Christ? This book helps to explain why this might be happening, and presents a convincing argument for why today's church services are mostly ineffective and inefficient. You will read concepts explained that you've not fully heard before. And you will get hints as to how it could, or should, work. –MikeM

Purchase the eBook for $4.99
Purchase the Paperback for $5.99

The Death and Resurrection of the Church

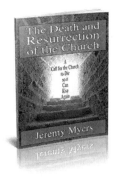

In a day when many are looking for ways to revitalize the church, Jeremy Myers argues that the church should die.

This is not only because of the universal principle that death precedes resurrection, but also because the church has adopted certain Satanic values and goals and the only way to break free from our enslavement to these values is to die.

But death will not be the end of the church, just as death was not the end of Jesus. If the church follows Jesus into death, and even to the hellish places on earth, it is only then that the church will rise again to new life and vibrancy in the Kingdom of God.

Reviews from Amazon

I have often thought on the church and how its acceptance of corporate methods and assimilation of cultural media mores taints its mission but Jeremy Myers eloquently captures in words the true crux of the matter—that the church is not a social club for do-gooders but to disseminate the good news to all the nooks and crannies in the world and particularly and primarily those bastions in the reign of evil. That the "gates of Hell" Jesus pronounces indicate that the church is a offensive, not defensive, posture as gates are defensive structures.

I must confess that in reading I was inclined to be in agreement as many of the same thinkers that Myers riffs upon have influenced me also—Walter Wink, Robert Farrar Capon, Greg Boyd, NT Wright, etc... So as I read, I frequently nodded my head in agreement. –GN Trifanaff

The book is well written, easy to understand, organized and consistent thoughts. It rightfully makes the reader at least think about things as… is "the way we have always done it" necessarily the Biblical or Christ-like way, or is it in fact very sinful?! I would recommend the book for pastors and church officers; those who have the most moving-and-shaking clout to implement changes, or keep things the same. –Joel M. Wilson

Purchase the eBook for $4.99
Purchase the Paperback for $8.99

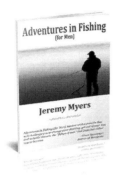

Adventures in Fishing (for Men)

Adventures in Fishing (for Men) is a satirical look at evangelism and church growth strategies.

Using fictional accounts from his attempts to become a world-famous fisherman, Jeremy Myers shows how many of the evangelism and church growth strategies of today do little to actually reach the world for Jesus Christ.

Adventures in Fishing (for Men) pokes fun at some of the popular evangelistic techniques and strategies endorsed and practiced by many Christians in today's churches. The stories in this book show in humorous detail how little we understand the culture that surrounds us or how to properly reach people with the Gospel of Jesus Christ. The story also shows how much time, energy, and money goes into evangelism preparation and training with the end result being that churches rarely accomplish any actual evangelism.

Reviews from Amazon

I found *Adventures in Fishing* (*For Men*) quite funny! Jeremy Myers does a great job shining the light on some of the more common practices in Evangelism today. His allegory gently points to the foolishness that is found within a system that takes the preaching of the Gospel and tries to reduce it to a simplified formula. A formula that takes what should be an organic, Spirit led experience and turns it into a gospel that is nutritionally benign.

If you have ever EE'd someone you may find Meyer's book offensive, but if you have come to the place where you realize that Evangelism isn't a matter of a script and checklists, then you might benefit from this light-hearted peek at Evangelism today. –Jennifer L. Davis

Purchase the eBook for $0.99

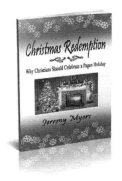

Christmas Redemption: Why Christians Should Celebrate a Pagan Holiday

Christmas Redemption looks at some of the symbolism and traditions of Christmas, including gifts, the Christmas tree, and even Santa Claus and shows how all of these can be celebrated and enjoyed by Christians as a true and accurate reflection of the Gospel.

Though Christmas used to be a pagan holiday, it has been redeemed by Jesus.

If you have been told that Christmas is a pagan holiday and is based on the Roman festival of Saturnalia, or if you have been told that putting up a Christmas tree is idolatrous, or if you have been told that Santa Claus is Satanic and teaches children to be greedy, then you must read this book! In it, you will learn that all of these Christmas traditions have been redeemed by Jesus and are good and healthy ways of celebrating the truth of the Gospel and the grace of Jesus Christ.

Reviews from Amazon

Too many times we as Christians want to condemn nearly everything around us and in so doing become much like the Pharisees and religious leaders that Jesus encountered.

I recommend this book to everyone who has concerns of how and why we celebrate Christmas.

I recommend it to those who do not have any qualms in celebrating but may not know the history of Christmas.

I recommend this book to everyone, no matter who or where you are, no matter your background or beliefs, no matter whether you are young or old. –David H.

Very informative book dealing with the roots of our modern Christmas traditions. The Biblical teaching on redemption is excellent! Highly recommended. –Tamara

Finally, an educated writing about Christmas traditions. I have every book Jeremy Myers has written. His writings are fresh and truthful. –Retlaw "Steadfast"

Purchase the eBook for $0.99

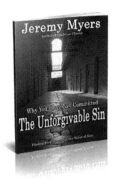

Why You Have not Committed the Unforgivable Sin: Finding Forgiveness for the Worst of Sins

Are you afraid that you have committed the unforgivable sin?

In this book, you will learn what this sin is and why you have not committed it. After surveying the various views about blasphemy against the Holy Spirit and examining Matthew 12:31-32, you will learn what the sin is and how it is committed.

As a result of reading this book, you will gain freedom from the fear of committing the worst of all sins, and learn how much God loves you!

Reviews from Amazon

This book addressed things I have struggled and felt pandered to for years, and helped to bring wholeness to my heart again. –Natalie Fleming

You must read this book. Forgiveness is necessary to see your blessings. So if you purchase this book, [you will have] no regrets. –Virtuous Woman

Jeremy Myers covers this most difficult topic thoroughly and with great compassion. –J. Holland

Good study. Very helpful. A must read. I like this study because it was an in depth study of the scripture. –Rose Knowles

Excellent read and helpful the reader offers hope for all who may be effected by this subject. He includes e-mails from people, [and] is very thorough. –Richie

Purchase the eBook for $4.99
Purchase the Paperback for $5.99

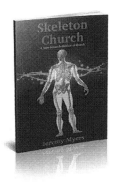

Skeleton Church: A Bare-Bones Definition of Church

The church has a skeleton which is identical in all types of churches. Unity and peace can develop in Christianity if we recognize this skeleton as the simple, bare-bones definition of church. But when we focus on the outer trappings—the skin, hair, and eye color, the clothes, the muscle tone, and other outward appearances—division and strife form within the church.

Let us return to the skeleton church and grow in unity once again.

Reviews from Amazon

My church gathering is struggling to break away from traditions which keep us from following Jesus into the world. Jeremy's book lends encouragement and helpful information to groups like us. –Robert A. White

I worried about buying another book that aimed at reducing things to a simple minimum, but the associations of the author along with the price gave me reason to hope and means to see. I really liked this book. First, because it wasn't identical to what other simple church people are saying. He adds unique elements that are worth reading. Second, the size is small enough to read, think, and pray about without getting lost. –Abel Barba

In *Skeleton Church*, Jeremy Myers makes us rethink church. For Myers, the church isn't a style a worship, a row of pews, or even a building. Instead, the church is the people of God, which provides the basic skeletal structure of the church. The muscles, parts, and flesh of the church are how we carry Jesus' mission into our own neighborhoods in our own unique ways. This eBook will make you see the church differently. –Travis Mamone

This book gets back to the basics of the New Testament church—who we are as Christians and what our perspective should be in the world we live in today. Jeremy cuts away all the institutional layers of a church and gets to the heart of our purpose as Christians in the world we live in and how to affect the people around us with God heart and view in mind. Not a physical church in mind. It was a great book and I have read it twice now. –Vaughn Bender

Purchase the eBook for $0.99

The Lie – A Short Story

When one billion people disappear from earth, what explanation does the president provide? Is he telling the truth, or exposing an age-old lie?

This fictional short story contains his televised speech.

Have you ever wondered what the antichrist will say when a billion people disappear from planet earth at the rapture? Here is a fictional account of what he might say.

Purchase the eBook for $0.99

Made in the USA
San Bernardino, CA
05 August 2018